Restoring Spirit

Belvia Holt Tate

authorHOUSE®

AuthorHouse™ LLC
1663 Liberty Drive
Bloomington, IN 47403
www.authorhouse.com
Phone: 1-800-839-8640

© 2013 Belvia Holt Tate. All rights reserved.

No part of this book may be reproduced, stored in a retrieval system, or transmitted by any means without the written permission of the author.

Published by AuthorHouse 12/03/2013

ISBN: 978-1-4918-2336-1 (sc)
ISBN: 978-1-4918-2334-7 (hc)
ISBN: 978-1-4918-2335-4 (e)

Library of Congress Control Number: 2013920683

Any people depicted in stock imagery provided by Thinkstock are models, and such images are being used for illustrative purposes only.
Certain stock imagery © Thinkstock.

This book is printed on acid-free paper.

Because of the dynamic nature of the Internet, any web addresses or links contained in this book may have changed since publication and may no longer be valid. The views expressed in this work are solely those of the author and do not necessarily reflect the views of the publisher, and the publisher hereby disclaims any responsibility for them.

Contents

Acknowledgements vii
Prologue xiii
My Family 1
Sit Up Straight 12
Darkness to Light 40
Yelling at God 58
Moving Mama 76
Empty Nest 90
Restoring Spirit 111
Recovering 136
Treasure Forever 157
Epilogue: August, 2007 167
Works Cited 171
About the Author 173
About the Book 175

Acknowledgements

I am forever grateful to so many individuals who have had great impact on my present state of mindfulness to God's plan in our lives. Thanks to all of you.

. . . to my parents, the late Carl and Shirley Holt, for being such great examples of keeping faith with God even in the worst of times . . .

. . . to my husband and daughter, Richard Tate and Loren Mitchell, for their unwavering love, support and encouragement . . .

. . . to my favorite brother and his wife, Glen and Nita Holt, who are always there for me . . .

. . . to my church family at Bedford Presbyterian Church for taking care of my family when I couldn't and for lifting me up to God in prayer; what a powerful presence you are in my life . . .

. . . to Reverend Joseph Gaston and his wife Karen, who have been instrumental in teaching me about God's grace and love, what it means to forgive and be forgiven, and how to see God in everything . . .

. . . to everyone at Peaks Presbyterian Pilgrimage 34 whose presence and insight would get me focused to write this book . . .

Belvia Holt Tate

. . . to Joyce Abbott Robertson and Reverend Marina Gopadze for their spiritual mentorship . . .

. . . to Reverend John Salley for using his English major to edit this text; your critique has been so helpful . . .

. . . to all my family and friends whose advice, help and love I could not live without . . .

Dearest Lord, teach me to be generous;
Teach me to serve thee as thou deservest;
To give and not count the cost,
To fight and not to heed the wounds,
To toil and not to seek the rest,
To labour and not to seek reward,
Save that of knowing that I do thy will.

*I dedicate this writing to the glory of
God by whose grace I am here.*

Prologue

The word spirit comes from the Latin origin of *spiritus,* meaning breath, courage, vigor, the soul, life.

"What lies behind us and what lies before us are tiny matters compared to what lies within us."
—Ralph Waldo Emerson

Our lives are much like water that flows down from a mountain, meandering willfully through the boulders in a stony creek bed. The water cascades over cliffs to pound pits into the sandy soil. There are lengths of flat shallow spaces where the water can rest for a time, comfortable in this place of refuge, getting used to this environment, familiar with this particular small area of the creek bed.

The water often stagnates, becoming too comfortable in that resting place with no movement forward. Then turbulence will appear from nowhere to flush the water out of its comfort zone. Crashing over the boulders, it spews through cracks and crevices too small to allow smooth passage.

There are shallow places along the way, filled with small rocks that cause the water to split without reason. Going in different directions, it quickly flows aimlessly here and there to eventually rejoin as one serene pool. Deep caverns can hold the water still for a long time, giving it opportunity to fathom its depths and gradually rise to the surface to warm in the sun and rejoin the flowing stream.

Life's trials are sometimes like being caught in a stagnant pool with fear and trepidation for what lies ahead. We can choose to stay mired up in that trial or move through it, with God's help, back to the main stream. We are given trials over and over during our lives and are allowed the choice of how we will get through them. We can either wallow in our misery or accept the challenge and ask God to lead us through. Ultimately that is the challenge . . . turning our lives over to God and accepting what he wills for us. Once admitting that we cannot do this alone, that only He is powerful enough to heal us, body and soul, only then will we experience the great joy and peace He can bring to our lives.

It took me fifty years of life to be able to do that, to admit that I could not make it through life anymore, physically or spiritually, without God to help me. What a joy and relief it has been to finally let God be the leader. I often think about all the time I've wasted, but the past is gone. We cannot change it, yet we can learn from our mistakes. I am so grateful that now I have a strong relationship with the Trinity of God . . . Father, Son, and Holy Spirit. It has been a long time in the making, but better late than never. Because of the chain of events that brought me to the gift of God's grace, it is all the more sweet now.

My Family

Daddy loved the place we lived. It really wasn't anything special. It was simply his place. Originally, the house was five rooms with an outhouse and smokehouse out back. The water had to be pumped from the well which was just off the back porch. This was all upgraded to six rooms with a bathroom and indoor plumbing before I was born. We had fifty-two acres of land, about eight to ten acres of which was pasture land along the Staunton River. This was often my favorite place to escape from Mama's ever watchful eyes. This particular piece of property was separated from the rest by fences and the Norfolk & Western railroad track. Mama would always make me promise not to walk the tracks before she would allow me to go down there. I say "down there" because the river road (as we called it) wound around and down a steep hill before reaching the track. Close to twenty acres of our land was wooded and very steep which made it virtually unusable except as a refuge for foxes, deer, squirrels, rabbits, quail, turkeys, and all the other wildlife calling south-central Virginia home. The pasture across the railroad tracks was longer than it was wide with the river on the long side opposite the railroad. Cows would be grazing in the sun. Huge sycamore, maple and oak trees along the river's bank assisted Daddy in making a fence so the cows could not cross the river. A small spring came from a pipe under the railroad tracks at the west end of the field where they could easily get a drink of water or lie down in the cool moss under the trees.

It was near that particular area that I claimed my favorite spot. My brother, Glen and his friend Jerry had shown it to me one day. The tree covered river bank was like a small cliff near where the spring fed into the river. If I climbed through the barbed wire fence, there was a narrow path that meandered down the bank. About half way down to the water, there was a wider shelf covered with moss. One of the trees further down the bank had a low branch that protruded like an "L" over the carpeted shelf. As a child, it was like having my own private little room where no one could find me. I would sit on the tree branch chair with my back against the upright part of the limb listening to the river flow by as I usually read a book. The only disturbance would be the lowing of the cows or having to smack at a big black ant that decided to taste me as it crawled by on the tree. As I grew a little older, it became my place to think, to try to figure out what life was all about and why things happened the way they did.

My father was usually a happy, good natured man, who loved to talk and swap tales with his friends. He had an easy smile on his face for everyone he met. He was one of those people who would talk to anybody. He never met a stranger who wasn't his friend before they parted. He loved God, family and country, in that order.

One of my earliest memories as a small child was sitting beside my father in church. He always had on a nice suit and a polished pair of wing tip shoes. His felt hat would be hanging at the back of the sanctuary on a hook. He was quite a handsome figure when he was all decked out for Sunday. Mama always made sure we were all clean and properly dressed to go to church. Our appearance was a reflection on her abilities as a homemaker and mother. We were not going to look like poor white people, even though we were. We had our everyday clothes and then we had our Sunday clothes. Mama made just about everything for all of us, except for Daddy. She made sure when he needed a new suit, it was good quality. She would look at all the seams and make sure it was put together right. Money was too hard to come by to waste it on a cheaply made suit. We children would get hand-me-downs sometimes from family and friends, but Mama made sure that if they were tattered at all that we didn't wear them in public.

I never knew Daddy to have more than three pair of shoes at any given time, but they were always wing tips. He had long narrow feet. If I remember correctly the size was 11 ½ AAA, which guaranteed a high price to purchase them. He had his work shoes, his Sunday shoes and his farming shoes. When his work shoes would wear out, he would go get a new pair of Sunday shoes and make his Sunday shoes his new work shoes. If the old work shoes had the least bit of life left in them, they would be worn to work the garden and milk the cow. If a hole wore into the sole, they would be taken to the shoe shop to be resoled. They were only thrown away when repair was impossible. My daddy definitely got his money's worth out of his wing tips. We children got one new pair of shoes a year which always seemed to coincide with going back to school. Our shoes were always purchased at least a half size too big, a whole size if Mama could make them stay on our feet, to give us some growing room so that we hopefully wouldn't have to get another pair before the start of the next school year. I remember having to stick tissues in the toes of my shoes when I was little to make them fit better until I grew into them.

Sometimes at church they would ask Daddy to pray during the worship service. It seemed to me the preacher would randomly pick someone to pray on Sunday morning. I would always lay down on the church pew about prayer time. I didn't want the preacher to see me and decide to call on me anytime soon. Yet, my daddy was always ready when he was asked. He would stand up, all tall and lanky, fold his hands on the back of the pew in front of us, and close his eyes. He didn't bow his head when he prayed aloud so that everyone could hear him. It was more like he closed his eyes in reverence and lifted his voice toward heaven. His deep resonant voice with a slow southern drawl, consistent with our south-central Virginia roots, would fill the sanctuary with the sounds of a man praying truly from his heart. I wish I could remember his prayers. I do remember how they would make me feel. I would close my eyes and rest my head on Mama's lap and let the sound of his voice lull me into a peaceful state. Years later, one of our family's closest friends told me that she just loved to hear my daddy pray. She said, "He could pray it all."

When other people would pray, that's when Daddy would bow his head. He always sat forward in the church pew and rested his head on his hands which were resting on the pew in front of him. I guess he felt that was the best way he could prostrate himself before the Lord without Mama getting embarrassed and making him get up and act like a gentleman.

On many Sundays there would be an altar call at the end of the worship service. This is when the preacher would ask anyone who believed Jesus Christ was their Savior and wanted to turn their life over to God to come forward to kneel at the altar. Daddy would always go up front to kneel down, put his folded arms on the altar and then rest his head on his arms. In a few minutes, Mama would go too. I would peek out from the pew into the aisle and look up front to see what was going on. Eventually, Daddy's back and shoulders would start shaking. He was crying as he always did when he went up front. Sometimes, a strange feeling would come over me. It wasn't frightening. It was just different. That is when I would get out into the aisle and walk up there to be with my parents. Daddy would take me in his arms and quietly sob until it was time to go outside after the service to shake hands with everybody and smoke a cigarette with his cronies under the big oak tree. It wasn't until I was older that I truly understood where my daddy's tears came from and why he would cling to me so tightly as he sobbed at the altar.

Whoever does not carry his own cross and come after me cannot be my disciple. (Luke 14:27, The Catholic Study Bible: New American Bible, New Testament p.128)

My father and mother, Carl and Shirley, were married on April 25, 1936. They both had jobs at the local weaving mill for a while. The first child was born to them ten months later in February 1937. Then another child came every four years after that until my parents stopped procreating in 1953. Mama didn't work publicly for too long after the children started coming. Daddy said it was cheaper for her to stay home with the children than work. He got a job as a rural letter carrier with the United States Postal Service and Mama became a housewife. I was the youngest of five children born to Carl and Shirley, the only girl with four big brothers. I grew up knowing one healthy brother, Glen, eight years older than me who would pick on me until I screamed at the top of my little lungs. Screaming was my only defense against a sibling so much older than me. I also knew my brother who was twelve years my senior, Dennis. He was quadriplegic, having had brain damage during his bouts with childhood diseases. Mama took care of Dennis at home for about four years after he became ill. Dennis was institutionalized because Mama was near the point of exhaustion and breakdown. We would go to see him every Sunday after lunch and sometimes bring him home for the weekend or maybe a week in the summer. It was hard work for my mother to take care of him while my daddy was at work, yet she did it without complaint and loved

Dennis dearly. She always talked about how smart he had been when he started school, a near genius she said. He looked like her, blond hair, fair complexion and ice blue eyes. Glen and I both knew growing up that Dennis was Mama's favorite child. He was the most helpless and needed her more than we did.

My other two brothers were unknown to me except through the stories my mother used to tell me as I was playing in the kitchen with her pots and pans or in the afternoons as she was trying to lull me to sleep for a nap. Roy was the first child born to my parents and sixteen years older. In the summer of 1943, Roy had his physical to start school which revealed anemia. The doctor gave him vitamins and iron to build up his blood and waited to give him his smallpox vaccination until he was stronger. Ten days before Christmas, the doctor felt he was better and gave him his vaccination. Whether it was from the anemia, some other blood disorder, or a rare allergy to the vaccination, we will never know; Roy died on December 31, 1943.

Dennis was two years old when Roy died and was still healthy at that point. Dennis didn't become ill until he started to school and got measles, mumps and chicken pox one right after the other. The high fevers caused him to have encephalitis, a swelling of the brain that damaged it and gradually made him a quadriplegic. Glen was just a toddler when that happened. My parents kept Dennis in school as long as they could but he gradually got to the point he was unable to do anything for himself, losing his dexterity and his ability to walk. During those early years of Dennis' gradual decline in health and also trying to rear a normal son, Carl and Shirley had a fourth son, Baxter.

Baxter was a beautiful baby boy. He was just like his father. He would look up at Mom with his big brown eyes and just laugh. He probably would have had black hair just like Carl if he had gotten old enough. Baxter died of double pneumonia when he was nine months old. He was buried on Christmas Day, 1949.

When I was little, Mama always told me how rich she would be if she had all her children. I always wanted to know why my parents wanted to keep having babies when so many bad things were happening to their children. Mama always said she kept trying for a girl. She told me the doctor said Glen was going to be a girl and if he had been, she probably wouldn't have had anymore children and Glen would have been named Belvia instead of Beverly Glen. But alas, Glen and Baxter were both boys and the girl didn't come along until number five. Finally Belvia, the girl child was born in May of 1953.

I don't remember the time when Dennis was living at home all the time. He was moved to a long-term care facility when I was two years old. But I do remember bringing him home for visits and I remember going to see him a lot with my parents. Glen was getting old enough to stay at home by himself while we went to see Dennis every Sunday. I sometimes got reprieve from the weekly trips by going home from church with my friends, Janet and Jane. While I loved seeing Dennis, it always made Mama so sad to say goodbye to him every week and Daddy was always really quiet on the way home. I found it much more pleasing to go home with Janet and Jane. Mildred, their mother, would fix lunch for us and send us off to play outside in the woods where Janet and Jane had swept out places in the dirt and marked off rooms with sticks. We would take our dolls and play house out there for hours. We were gourmet mud pie makers. If it was raining we would stay inside and cut paper dolls out of Sears Roebuck catalogs, play Monopoly all afternoon in the basement, or dress up Janet's Barbie doll.

Yet, there were some good times during those visits to see Dennis. Dennis and Glen always called me Sister for as long as I can remember. Dennis' brain development had stopped at about the age of an eight year old. Mama would always ask him who I was when he would first see me. He always knew, calling me Soos-ta. Mama would take something to feed Dennis while we visited like homemade tapioca pudding, which he dearly loved, or a piece of cake she had made on Saturday morning. Sometimes we would get to take him outside for a while if it was sunny and warm.

There was another patient at the facility, a man who always sat with Dennis during the day. He would always talk to Dennis and yell (and I mean that literally) for the nurses if Dennis needed anything. His name was Jimmy. My guess is that he was in his thirties. He was slightly retarded, but not really so much that he couldn't have taken care of himself. His condition was made worse because he had been blind for some reason since childhood. We always took him a serving of whatever we had for Dennis to eat. If we took Dennis outside or for a ride in the car on those Sunday afternoons, we always let Jimmy come along. I remember one of the nurses saying once that his family lived in another state and only visited two or three times a year. He had attached himself to Dennis and our family as soon as Dennis was moved to his area of the campus.

When I was about ten years old, Jimmy received an eye donor's bequest to have transplants for his eyes and the surgery would be paid for as well. Jimmy was going to be able to see for the first time in many, many years. We were so happy for him and he was so excited. He so much wanted to be able to finally see his family he had adopted.

There was a visiting room at the front of Dennis' building where they always took us and brought Dennis to see us. The nurse would always bring Jimmy, too. Several weeks went by while Jimmy had his surgery and recovery that we did not see him. Finally, Jimmy's big day to see us, really see us, was here. He had big brown framed thick glasses on his small face as he walked in. I said, "Hi Jimmy!" His face lit up into the biggest smile I have ever seen. He knew who I was from my voice. He turned to me and took my face in his hands and said, "Oh Soos-ta, I can see you!" Tears of joy rolled down his cheeks and mine. I knew at that moment I was seeing one of God's miracles I had been hearing about at church. He sat with us that day so elated about his ability to see. It was such a treat to see joy in this place of so little hope.

A few months after Jimmy regained his sight, one of his sisters was able to provide a place in her home for him to live. Again we saw the joyful tears of Jimmy's happiness as we said our good-byes, hugged him and watched him ride away to his new home to be a part of his real family again. Yet, even though we were happy for him to start his new seeing life, we were saddened by his loss to us, especially to Dennis. Dennis never had another companion like Jimmy to keep him company everyday or look after his every need. Within a year after losing Jimmy to his new life, we lost Dennis, too. He was buried with his two other brothers on March 3, 1964 at the age of 21. At that time, Glen was in college and I was almost eleven.

Through all of this tragedy in their lives, my parents never lost their faith in God. They both always said that they never would have made it through all that happened, losing those boys, if God had not helped them through it. They never questioned why these things were happening to them. They just believed that God was the Almighty, creator and giver of life. They didn't question why he did things the way he did. They just knew that everything was His will and God would help them deal with it.

Around that same time, we had a young minister in our church who took more of an interest in the youth. He had gotten a minister who was involved with inner city kids to speak at our yearly church revival that spring. Every night the minister would get the youth of the church to come up front, then tell us stories about how some of the worst drug abusing, downtrodden young people in the inner city had been brought to Christ. I was fascinated by his stories. He was telling us about a world that I never knew existed. Shortly after that, all of our parents sent us to a class that our minister gave on the church and baptism. All of us in the class were about the same age. When the class was over we were all asked if we were ready to join the church and be baptized. We all enthusiastically agreed and proceeded to be baptized at the same service. I'm not sure that any of us really felt led to it, but it seemed to me that it was the right thing to do at the time. Everybody else was doing it. I didn't want to feel left out and I surely didn't want to go to hell if I was the next one of Carl and Shirley's kids to die and never have been baptized. While I went through the motions, it didn't really feel like I thought it would. I thought I would get that strange feeling again like I did before I would go up to the altar with Daddy. It didn't happen and I was confused.

Not long after my baptism, I was starting to question the God of love that everybody at church kept talking about. Why was he allowing such turmoil in our lives? Nobody else's children were dying like the ones in my family. Why were my parents so devout to God, who seemed so unrelenting in letting bad things happen? If He controlled all, why couldn't He fix everything bad and make it good. Weren't parents supposed to die first and not see their children suffer? When I would ask Mama about it, she would lower her shaking head and just say, "I don't know, honey. It's just God's will." If I said anything to Daddy about my questions, he would emphatically say, "You are not to question anything to do with God or His will in our lives. You just need to believe and know that God sent Jesus Christ to die on the cross for our sins and that it is He who controls our lives."

I thought to myself, "Well, that really clears things up for me, Daddy." I suppose this mode of explanation came partly out of the time in social history where women were still more subservient to men and didn't need to have questions answered. Women should just believe what men told them and that was that. My inquisitive nature often perturbed Daddy. If a situation or conversation was getting out of my father's control, he would become irritated and short to shut me up. Daddy never in his life struck me, but his tongue could sometimes cut deep into my soul. My father's short responses to my questions about God, faith or life never failed to make me feel I must be too ignorant to understand. In reflection, I don't think this was my father's intention, but perhaps a defense mechanism because these were unanswered questions he also contemplated. Perhaps Daddy was afraid to question. He just wanted to bear his cross and be a disciple of Jesus, no questions necessary.

Sit Up Straight

To harness the power of water to generate electricity, Appalachian Power Company had decided to build two dams along the Stanton River. Northwest of us the river was called Roanoke. When Daddy first heard about it, he hoped they would build one of them down stream from our farm. Our unusable land would become a cove and our good land would become lakefront property. After all the meetings, hearings, and uproar of people who would lose their homes, dams were built at Leesville, four miles upriver from us and Smith Mountain, further to the northwest. The building of these two dams and holding back water to fill the two lakes that they created wreaked havoc on our river bank property. Holding back the water made our banks dry out. When the water was finally released to restore river flow downstream, the waters washed our dried riverbanks away. Over a short period of time, the sycamores, maples, and oaks along the bank had fallen over into the river. The barbed wire fence was gone. Instead of sloping banks leading to the water, now the top layer of land jutted out over where the water had washed away the earth underneath. Instead of lake front property, Daddy got a thousand dollars for land acreage lost, a pittance for the beauty and solitude now gone.

Just like the time when I was about four years old and Mama threw away Baby Annie because I carried her around by her arm and it came off, this loss rocked me in a spiritual way. Daddy was also devastated by the loss of the riverbanks that he loved so much. I think he would rather them have amputated his leg. I felt the same. My beautiful moss covered shelf with the tree branch chair was floating downstream to the Chesapeake Bay along with my childhood.

Daddy always said that God wouldn't give you more than you could handle. I wasn't so sure about that. He sure was giving me more that I wanted to deal with and I most certainly didn't know how to handle it.

In the spring of 1965, almost a year to the day after Dennis's death, I got a bad cold that I couldn't get over. Mama took me to see our long time family physician, Dr. Shreve. His office in town was in a narrow white stucco two story building. The windows in the front downstairs made a corner with glass block that you couldn't see through. To get to Dr. Shreve's office you opened a door and walked straight up a dark, steep narrow staircase that looked and felt like it had a hundred steps to climb. It was a blessing that Dr. Shreve made house calls when necessary, because there is no way someone feeble, overweight, or very ill could have made it up that staircase.

The office was just a long hallway with rooms on one side and the ends of it. As you topped the stairs, the secretary's office was across the hall. To the left the first room always had the door shut. This made the hallway look dark and dingy at the top of the stairs. I found out in later years that Dr. Shreve's office was behind the closed door, filled with his medical books, personal military mementos from WWII, and pictures of his wife and children. It was a warm and cozy room with comfortable leather chairs and a mahogany desk. The waiting room was to the right and the last door on the left. This room was always filled with crying babies, congested coughers, smokers, chatty mothers and misbehaving children. A long wait to see the doctor was the norm. There was no appointment schedule; it was first come, first serve. Everybody that was in the waiting room when you arrived would be seen before you were. Mama would always tell me to sit down, get comfortable and hand me a children's Highlight magazine, even when I was a teenager.

After our customary wait with continuous count downs to see how many people were here before our arrival, we finally were called back to one of the three examining rooms. These rooms were on the other end of the hall, to the left of the staircase landing. The sun was usually shining on the front side of the building in the afternoon and those rooms always seemed brighter and more inviting, except for the bright room at the end of the hall. As a child, I had always hated being put in that room because it was also the office pharmacy. The nurses were always coming in mixing medications for injections. I would sit on the examining table waiting for the doctor with my arms crossed and my hands covering the area on my arms just below my shoulders where I always got shots. The nurses were Katherine and Clara. Katherine went to our church and would always make Clara give me shots when I had to have them so I wouldn't think badly of her when I saw her every Sunday. Katherine helped me to learn how to knit and I always thought Clara must be Florence Nightingale. Whenever seen on the street in her nursing uniform, she was starched from head to toe from her cap to her pinafore hem. Her black hair was pulled into a tight bun at the back of her neck. The polished white shoes accented every step as her navy blue wool cape floated in the breeze.

Clara took me and Mama into the room to the right of the office pharmacy. It was a corner room and had two windows. It was the brightest room on the hall and had the best view of the busy street

Restoring Spirit

below. Dr. Shreve strolled in smiling with chart and pen in hand greeting us with hugs as he was prone to do.

As he examined me, he noticed something different about my back. He said, "Belvia, sit up straight."

"I am sitting up straight, Dr. Shreve."

Mama scolded, "Belvia, don't talk ugly to Dr. Shreve. Do what he says and sit up straight."

"I am, Mama," I said beseechingly.

Dr. Shreve put up his hand to quiet Mama, since she was about to backhand me into the next room. "Here Belvia, pull your blouse up in the back to your neck so I can get a good look at you." To Mama's great relief, I finally did what I was told. Dr. Shreve rubbed his hand down my back, then moved his fingers down my spine. He was very quiet for a minute. "Hmmmm, Belvia let me help you down from that table and stand up here on the floor in front of my stool." Again, I did as I was told. He wanted me to take off everything but my panties so he could see by back better. I gave Mama a strange look because he had never asked me to do such a thing before. She looked worried but comforted me by telling me it was alright and helped me get undressed. Dr. Shreve sat down on the stool behind me and put his hands on my shoulders like he was trying to be sure I was straight across. He put his hands at my waist and pushed in at the top of my pelvis. He made me bend forward and rubbed down my back again. He then turned me to each side and placed his hand flat against my back, moving it up and down from my neck to my waist several times. This wasn't so bad. I really liked back rubs.

Of course, by the time he turned me to the side the second time, Mama was getting jumpy. "What are you looking at, Dr. Shreve."

"Have you noticed anything different about the way Belvia sits or walks or how her clothes fit?"

"Not really, I'm always telling her to sit up straight and not slouch in the chair when she is watching television. She and her brother both like to sit sideways in that old chair in the living room, throwing their legs over the arm on the side. I've told them both a thousand times not to do it."

Dr. Shreve quickly came to my and my brother's defense, letting Mama know that this was not something caused by us hanging our legs over the arm of the living room chair. He proceeded to tell Mama that it looked like I had a slight curvature of the spine and he wanted me to see a specialist in orthopedics about it. The specialist would do some x-rays of my back and see just what was what. He reassured us that everything would be alright and he would get everything set up.

That night Mama told Daddy all about our visit to Dr. Shreve at the supper table. He didn't have much to say at dinner and took a walk to the river afterwards saying he was going to check on the cows. He was gone a long time. Mama shut herself in their bedroom and I could hear her crying while I tried to do my homework. Nothing more was mentioned about it until they kept me out of school one day in the fall to go see the specialist in the city.

Thus, I heard the word *scoliosis* for the first time. Over the next two years my parents took me to physical therapy every week, the doctor every month. I did exercises every day and listened to Mama tell me to sit up straight another thousand times. There were tons of x-rays taken. Dr. Jones, the orthopedic surgeon, would mark them up with a grease pencil and write measurements on them. The curvature located in my thoracic spine slowly continued to progress. Twelve, thirteen, fourteen degrees . . . seventeen, eighteen, nineteen degrees. Dr. Jones told us if it reached twenty degrees he would need to do surgery.

Restoring Spirit

In the spring of 1964, Glen finished his electronics program at Danville Technical Institute and got a job with General Electric in Lynchburg. Things so far had gone pretty well for him. He had done well in school and gotten a good paying job. He was strong and healthy. He was out on his own, the first and only child of five to reach adulthood without major incident. At least Carl and Shirley had one child they didn't have to worry about . . . . except for the draft.

Glen had been deferred from the military draft while he was still going to school, but now that he had completed his education his number could come up at any time. Vietnam was a hotbed of death and my strong, healthy brother would surely have to go if he got drafted. In January of 1966, Glen left for boot camp in Georgia. He was in the Army now for his required two years of military service.

During the time I was having my physical therapy sessions and being x-rayed prolifically, Glen was being trained to operate and maintain an amphibious vessel at two different Army bases near Virginia Beach. At least he was back in our home state now, but being sent on tour in Vietnam transporting supplies from ship to shore was eminent. We felt at least there was a glimmer of hope. He would not be in the jungles or the rice paddies fighting the Viet Cong face to face. In November 1966, we said our tearful goodbyes to Glen as he left for Cam Rahn Bay, Vietnam. Mama wrote Glen every day of the week except Saturday. The only reason she didn't write that day was because Joe, Daddy's co-worker and our mailman, didn't pick up the mail on Sunday to take it to the post office. I would send a letter every week or so and keep Glen posted on the progress of the high school football team who had not beaten our arch rival in thirteen years. Mama and I would make "care packages" every few weeks to send goodies to him. We made brownies and cookies and sent packs of raisins. *Raisin* became Glen's nickname in Vietnam because he had moles on his shoulders and back that looked like raisins and we would send him those raisins in our packages. His buddies couldn't believe that Raisin was not his nickname already. He said some of his buddies didn't get much from home so he would share his letters and packages with them. I remember writing some letters to his friends too. I became Raisin's crazy sister to all of them. Glen would write home regularly and Mama would go down to meet Joe at the mail box every day in anticipation of getting his letters. It seemed to give her relief from worry, if only temporarily. She knew at least Glen was safe at the time he wrote the letter. He wrote of funny things that would happen between him and his friends and told us he was contributing to the war effort by transporting ice cream from ship to shore. He never once wrote of having to do any type of combat activity. I knew even if he did, he wouldn't tell us so Mama and Daddy wouldn't worry so much.

Walter Cronkite and the CBS News were a daily part of our lives. Mama and Daddy were always sitting in their designated spots in the living room to watch the news every night. The tension was mounting in Vietnam as well as here at home. As more men died or became prisoners of war, the more people started protesting our presence there. Five months after Glen went to Vietnam he was told he was being transferred to Thailand to transport ammunition. He wasn't sure of the exact date for that to happen, but he would keep us posted. Near that same time, Dr. Jones was trying to convince my parents that I needed to have a spinal fusion to put a halt to my spinal curve progression. I had hit twenty degrees in my curvature about the time Glen left for Vietnam. It took Dr. Jones and Mama several months to talk Daddy into letting me have it done. Once Daddy finally agreed to it, there was much work to be done to prepare for the surgery and recovery time. It was agreed that I would have the surgery on Memorial Day, 1967, just days after my fourteenth birthday. I would only miss a week of school at the end of the eighth grade and hopefully would be back on my feet when school started again in the fall.

I then had to be fitted for a brace to wear for six months after I got out of the post surgical cast. I would inhabit the cast from my armpits to my knees, in bed, flat on my back for the three months of summer. I had really never felt that I was deformed so that anybody would really notice until I had to be fitted for that brace. I was being a guinea pig for the prosthetic device maker who was working with Dr. Jones to manufacture a brace that would hold my spine in place and not allow me to give into the curve of my spine while at the same time allowing me to be mobile enough to go to school.

What a monstrosity that brace turned out to be. It had a plastic type corset that fit around my pelvis with a leather tongue so that it could be strapped to my pelvis like tying a tennis shoe with Velcro straps, only there was no such thing as Velcro then. The straps were quarter inch thick, one inch wide cotton fabric strips secured in place after pulling them as hard as possible with a metal toothed clip. Attached to that plastic girdle were metal bars in the form of the U shaped nails Daddy used to attach the barbed wire to the fence posts. Those were turned upside down in the front and back rising up to about the level of the top of my sternum. The doctor and designer wanted to pull my rib cage from right to left. The right side of my ribs in the back was humping out as my spine curved. Thus they fashioned another piece of plastic formed to the right side of my chest that could be connected to the back bar and then strapped around the front bar to pull as tightly to the left as possible. It also was held in place by another metal toothed clip. As if that wasn't enough to torture me with, they wanted my left shoulder to be raised to extend the left side of my rib cage which was caving in from the curvature. After several types of additions to the left side of the brace without satisfaction for

Dr. Jones, the prosthetic designer came up with an idea that pleased the good doctor, but did nothing to promote the self esteem of a budding young teenager. A third piece of plastic was molded to fit my left upper arm. This was attached to the metal bars to the left side of the brace, to protrude perpendicular to my body. Up until this point, I was not particularly distressed about being able to hide this brace under my clothes. Mama had always made my clothes and was perfecting ways to hide my deformity by taking up my skirts at the right waist band to make my hem look straight. I would wear pull over sweaters over them. She made me dresses that didn't have waist bands. Shift style jumpers were the rage back then and tent dresses were coming into vogue. But there was no hem adjustment or dress style that was going to hide my left arm sticking straight out from my body from my shoulder to my elbow with the rest of my arm hanging straight down from that. No amount of crying was going to change Dr. Jones mind about this design. It would do exactly what he wanted done. I would be a pioneering example for the medical books to help future generations of scoliosis patients. I did not give a hoot about being in the medical books. I just wanted this nightmare to be over.

While the brace design was taking on its monstrous shape, Walter Cronkite came into our living room one night as he had done many nights before. Yet, this night would be different. This night his news report struck a chord of fear in the hearts of my family that made everything else we were dealing with seem trivial. Cronkite's voice boomed on the television in our living room that Cam Rahn Bay had been bombed. The main port in South Vietnam for receiving supplies for our troops was severely damaged. The death toll was uncertain. The three of us were struck silently numb with this news. That is where Glen still was stationed. As of his last letter that we had gotten the day before, he had not been moved to Thailand and still was unsure of when that would occur. My mother suddenly burst into tears and stood up, screaming at the top of her lungs and shaking her fist in the air, "God, how can you take another son from me? Why do you have to have them all? Can't you leave me just one?" Daddy jumped up and grabbed her to him as she beat upon his chest, still screaming and crying. Tears welled in my eyes as they are now while I write this. I too got up and hugged Mama and Daddy, trying to comfort them by letting them know I was still there for them. Finally, after what seemed like hours of standing there, the three of us hugging each other, Daddy finally said, "We don't know for sure that Glen was killed or injured. There is always hope that he was shipped to Thailand before the bombing. It's been two weeks since his last letter was written. A lot could have happened in two weeks. Glen will write us as soon as he can. Have faith in the good Lord to protect him and bring him back to us."

It was already time for another letter to come from Glen. He had always been diligent to send a letter at least every two weeks, sometimes more. Every day Mama would meet Joe at the mail box to see if there was a letter. Joe told us later he hated to come to our mailbox empty handed. Mama was trying so hard to be hopeful, yet everyday he had to shake his head to let her know there was no letter from Glen. Mama would silently turn away and walk back up the hill to the house with her head held high and tears streaming down her face.

A month had passed since the news of the Cam Rahn Bay bombing. Daddy kept trying to keep Mama together by telling her that no news was good news. The government had not sent a soldier to knock on our door. We were always glued to the television with Cronkite every night hoping to get more news of what was happening or maybe actually see Glen on the television. The news was always about more of our boys being killed or missing in action. We were losing hope of ever seeing Glen again. One Saturday morning, a few weeks before my surgery was scheduled, Joe rolled up our driveway. He didn't see Mama but saw that the kitchen door was open through the closed-in back porch. He knew she was home and started blowing his car horn in long, loud burst. Mama was washing breakfast dishes at the kitchen sink and heard the horn blowing outside. She walked to the kitchen door to see what was going on. There, in his muddy mail route car at our backdoor was Joe, blowing his horn enough to wake the dead and waving an airmail envelope out of his car window for Mama to see. What a glorious site to see Joe waving that letter from Glen, beckoning her to come see that her son was still alive and well in Thailand. Daddy had already opened the letter and read it at the post office when Joe found it sorting his mail that morning. Daddy wanted to call Mama and tell her the good news. Joe would not have it. "Carl Holt, I have had to turn that woman away from the mail box every day for a month. You are going to let me get the joy of delivering this letter to her personally." When Mama saw Joe waving that letter she screamed that high pitched squeal of happiness she always emitted when she won a hand of Rook and came running to get her hands on that letter. Joe did get out of the car before Mama got to him, but barely. She grabbed the letter and was hugging and kissing Joe like he had personally saved Glen's life. Daddy drove up just after that and always said that he didn't know what would have happened if he hadn't showed up to get Mama off of poor old Joe. Of course, I woke up with all the horn blowing and looked out my bedroom window about the time Daddy was pulling Mama from her lip lock on Joe. They were all hugging each other, jumping up and down, laughing and crying at the same time. I didn't even need to be told my only brother was alright. The vision I saw from the window was all I needed. Remembering it now once again brings tears of joy and relief to my eyes. It was the first time in many months that I had heard my mother's famous happy squeal and for just as long seen that easy smile of Daddy's on his face.

During these stressful times in the life of my family, my parents became more and more protective of me. Because of my back problems, they wouldn't allow me to participate in any extra curricular activities before the surgery for fear of my getting hurt. I was even discouraged from signing up for chorus again at school for the following school year which would be after I had my surgery, for fear I wouldn't be well enough or able enough to participate. I know it was unintentional on my parents part, but this was when I started feeling the twinges of self doubt, that I really was different from everyone else, that I wasn't good enough, that I was deformed. While they were trying to protect me from the possibility of failure, they were making me feel that I would never be able to succeed on my own.

The surgery went well except for a sudden drop in my blood pressure at one point that freaked out everyone in the operating room. When Dr. Jones told my parents what had happened, Daddy's blood pressure went through the roof and they had to lay him down in the floor of the lobby of the hospital and treat his high blood pressure so he wouldn't have a stroke. Once everybody got over that first week after my surgery, of Daddy's blood pressure fluctuations, and my vomiting from the anesthesia, I spent the rest of that summer fairly uneventfully, flat on my back in a cast from my armpits to my knees. I would stay in bed until Daddy got home from work about three o'clock in the afternoon. He would then pick me up by grabbing my cast just under my neck and the bar that had been placed across my knees and hoist me to a chaise lounge with wheels on it and move me to the living room where there was an air-conditioning unit in the window or outside to breathe some fresh air. I worked puzzles until they were no longer a challenge. I read <u>The Count of Monte Cristo</u> and <u>The Hobbit</u>. Someone lent us a television to use in my bedroom that would only pick up one channel. Everyday I watched reruns of *The Fugitive* until I knew them all by heart. Some days my friends would come over and stay with me while Mama would get out of the house to shop or go to the grocery store. I always loved those summer days even though I couldn't move around much. The girls would fill me in on all the gossip in the teenage world. We would listen to our favorite Motown records or harmonize to the latest Beatles release. Jip, who was the father of one of Daddy's best friends, was retired and would walk from the small town we lived near to our house once a week to bring me a carton of Cokes and some ice cream. Sundays would bring hordes of visitors, family and friends who couldn't come to visit during the week. Everyone who knew my family or knew of us was taking care of us, bringing food, sending money. I felt like a queen during that summer. Our little town made sure I wanted for nothing.

The time finally came for the cast to be removed. When Dr. Jones got it sawed off of me and put the magnificently designed brace on my body, it no longer fit. I had lost weight because I had no appetite lying on my back all day and night for three months. Mama even had Dr. Shreve give me some kind of tonic to supposedly make me hungrier. I could never convince her that the tonic only made it worse. It tasted nasty and made me nauseous so that I didn't want to eat. I often wondered if she really bought it from one of those snake oil and elixir sales men who traveled through the towns in the old Wild West movies. I could envision some guy with one of those big starched collars and paisley print cravats; his hair slicked down and parted in the middle. He would be standing on the back of his painted wagon, twirling his handle bar mustache with one hand and with the other hand holding the tonic bottle out for Mama to see while he told her how this wonderful elixir would cure everything that ailed me. From this recollection of my imagination, I must have thought my mother was pretty gullible to be convinced by our snake oil salesman, Dr. Shreve, that his elixir would make me eat. At any rate, the weight loss caused the prosthetic maker to have to make new body molds to remake the brace for me to wear when I got out of the cast. I had to go back into another full body cast until they could remake a brace to fit. I was devastated by this news even though it was only going to be for a week to ten days. It would throw me behind getting back on my feet and learning to walk again. I was not going to be allowed to put my feet on the floor without that brace on my body. I was not only going to have to go back to school with my arm sticking out like a sore thumb, I was going to have to start late, bringing more attention to my disability and deformity.

The new brace was made in a week; the cast was removed. This time at least the brace fit correctly, although it had not gotten any less conspicuous. I was bound and determined to get back on my feet as soon as possible, get back in school with my friends so I could be guaranteed of graduating with the people I had grown up with. I had no desire to add insult to injury by having to skip a year of school. With perseverance I succeeded. I was a week late starting my freshman year of high school, but I succeeded in catching up quickly. I couldn't take the stairs yet and my friends graciously carried my books to my classes for me while I walked outside of the building to go from one floor to the other. I will always be grateful to those friends who worked diligently to make my life bearable during those six months. My homeroom and locker were in the farthest western corner of the quarter mile long hallway on the only floor on that end of the building. All my classes were in the eastern half of the building with a first floor and a basement of classrooms. My classes were one upstairs and the next downstairs. The only time I could get to my locker was during lunch when I had to go back to the western end of the building to eat in the cafeteria. I was always late for class. I would sometimes hear people say to their friends after I had passed them in the hall, "Why has that girl got her arm sticking out like that? It looks ridiculous." or "What's wrong with her?" The more I heard comments like this, the more determined I became to get through this unscathed. Those people would be amazed when I looked like Miss America and wouldn't give them the time of day. I refused to let them get to me. Eventually I got stronger to the point that I could still go out of the building to go to my next class and not be late. Dr. Jones finally told me after a couple of months that I could start trying the stairs. I was very happy about that because it was getting cold outside.

My parents were still being very protective of me. Ball games were not allowed unless Daddy went with me to make sure the crowds didn't throw me to the ground and trample me to death in a stampede. Most of the time, I just didn't go. I thought Mama was going to have a heart attack when I fell down the stairs at school and broke the arm piece off my brace. She had a fit because I didn't lay there on my back at the bottom of the stairs and have her called immediately to come get me. Instead, I had merely gotten up with the arm piece in hand and went to class. She was to pick me up in an hour anyway. She hauled me to Dr. Jones office as soon as I got in the car and told her what had happened. He told her I would have to wait until the next afternoon to get it back from being repaired. I should stay home from school and not overdo it, but it would be alright for me to sit in a chair, or walk in the house. She made me stay in the bed until she got my brace back the next afternoon. The only time she would let me get up was to go to the bathroom . . . with supervision!! She had to wait to go pick up my brace after Daddy got home from work so I wouldn't be left alone to wander around the house without my brace. When I told Daddy what Dr. Jones had said and how excessive Mama was being about me moving around the house he just said, "Just do what your mama says." She forbade me from using the stairs anymore after that, but I did and just didn't tell her. I decided I would come up with some other story to tell her how I broke my brace if I fell down the stairs again. Daddy wasn't going to intercede in my defense, so I was on my own.

I fought a lot with my parents trying to get them to lighten up and give me a little freedom. All I still wanted was to be treated like a normal girl, not like some fragile piece of crystal that would break if touched. My only hope at this point was that Glen was supposed to come home near the end of November. At least maybe I would have an understanding ally in my brother. We all waited in anticipation of Glen's return, but no one prayed harder than I did for his safe return home.

The fall of that year was especially chilly. The leaves had already turned their brilliant display of color and fallen to the ground. Every morning starting at the end of October, I would check the calendar that was nailed to the back of the kitchen door trying to estimate how many more days there were until Glen might be home. We didn't know the exact date, but we had projected his twelve months stint overseas would be over by November 30. Glen and I had fought like cats and dogs when we were kids, but now we had both gone through what we hoped were the worst times of our lives without each other. I knew things would get better if only Glen would come home.

I had made a new friend at school that year. We always called each other by our last names; her name was Burnette. She was from a tobacco farming family near the town our high school was located. She was in my homeroom and all of my classes. We started walking to class together, eating lunch together, and hanging out in the hall talking to our friends when we had the chance. We became best friends. Mama and Daddy were always really picky about who my friends were. I couldn't be associated with anyone of questionable heritage. It didn't matter what the character of the friend was, if their mother or father were known to be of ill repute, the friendship was off limits. Of course, I would argue that my friends should not bear the brunt of their parents' sins. Mama would always respond, "Naught from naught, naught remains." We laugh about Mama's logic now, but it was an infuriating response for a teenage girl to hear. As it turned out, Burnette was deemed to be of good standing because a girl, who had grown up in our church, had married one of Burnette's brothers. The father of this girl vouched for the family and my friendship with Burnette was allowed to flourish with my parents' blessing. We became inseparable.

Most of my other girlfriends were starting to have boyfriends and go to dances. On Saturday nights, there was always a dance in the basement of Jimmy's Restaurant in the small town next to ours. This was another one of my restrictions. Mama said, "Good girls don't go to those kinds of dances." I never knew what kinds of dances were going on there to make them so disgusting to my parents, but all my other friends went and were what I considered good girls. It really didn't matter to me though, because nobody was going to want to dance with me in this contraption with my arm sticking out. Burnette didn't care about going to those dances either, so we would either get together at her house or mine or talk on the telephone.

Mama had been driving the twelve miles twice a day to take me to school and pick me up. I had arranged to have two study halls that year so I could get most of my homework done at school and not have to take so many books home. Three days a week, I had study hall the first period and last period of the day. On Tuesdays and Thursdays I was allowed to leave at one o'clock, since on those days my study halls were both at the end of the day.

This particular Tuesday morning during the first week in November was no different than any other. I got out of bed, of course not standing up without putting that confounded brace on and got dressed for school in some baggy dress Mama had made me to hide the brace, knee socks and a pair of saddle oxford shoes which were again in style at the time. Mine were beige with a darker brown saddle . . . very cool. I ate a bowl of Cheerios with lots of milk and sugar for breakfast and got my books to the car. Mama and I rode the twelve miles together like we had done every day since the middle of September, her usually telling me how she always wrote her papers perfectly and that I should work harder to make better grades in history. I spent that time wishing I could ride the bus again with the kids from our neighborhood that I had grown up with, talking and laughing all the way to school. When she dropped me off, she said her usual, "See you at one" and drove away.

At one o'clock the bell rang for class to be over. I was especially excited about Mama picking me up today. I had gotten an A on the paper I had written for history. Maybe this would get her off my back about my grades and her perfection in her school work. I had already been to my locker at lunch and gotten my books sorted out to take home. Burnette said she would take my history book and put it in her locker later since I didn't need it. Having the same schedule as I did, Mr. McKeever, our study hall teacher, told Janet she could help me get my books to the car before she came to class on the days I left early. Mama opened the door from the inside of Glen's car, the navy blue Oldsmobile Cutlass convertible that we had been using as a second car while Glen was gone. We thanked Burnette for her assistance as we always did and Mama pointed the car in the direction of home. She was fairly quiet as we drove home. I guess she couldn't get a word in edgewise since I was rattling on and on about my history paper. But she was smiling, so I took that as a good sign that she was pleased with my accomplishment. We were about half-way home when she said to me, "Guess what?"

"I don't know, Mama, maybe you're proud of me?"

"Glen got home this morning."

"What?" I didn't believe what I heard. "He's not due in for at least another three weeks."

"He pecked on the back door about ten o'clock this morning. He said his commanding officer came by a couple of days ago and told them to get their gear together and be on the runway in one hour. The *Freedom Bird,* what the soldiers called the plane that took guys back to the States, would be there to take them home. They were officially discharged from the United States Army." The next five or six miles home seemed to take hours. Of all things, Mama had to stop at the grocery store on the way to pick up some cheese. "Your brother came in the door and all he wanted to eat was a cheese sandwich and I didn't have any. We are going to stop and get that boy some cheese and have grilled cheese sandwiches for Glen's coming home dinner." I thought it would take forever.

My history paper long forgotten, I prepared myself to be reunited with my only brother. Mama had told me not to be surprised, that Glen was awfully thin. The jungle heat and bad food had not done him any favors. He had also been nursing a toothache and abscessed tooth that he was not going to let any jack leg Army dentist in Thailand jerk out. He had been eating aspirins like candy for two weeks. What seemed to be Mama's lifetime mission and talent, to take care of everybody, was once again in motion. "Don't you worry one little bit. We'll get his tooth fixed and get him fattened back up again in no time."

Glen's aspirin use and the fact that he had come from temperatures of 120 degrees in the shade to a cool 50 degrees during the day and the mid to low 30's at night were making him feel like he was freezing. When I walked into the living room, the oil floor furnace was cranking out enough heat to get the house to 100 degrees in a hurry. Glen was curled up on the couch with a coat on and two of Mama's handmade quilts wrapped around him. I will never forget the gaunt look on his face when he sat up to greet me. The only other one of Mama's children to inherit her ice blue eyes, his looked sunken into his head, dark circles ringing them. His skin was brown from the sun, but he seemed to have no color, almost like he was on a black and white TV show. His face was extremely thin, his hair very short. I don't remember ever seeing him that thin. His ears and beak nose that he had also inherited from Mama's side of the family seemed to stick out larger than normal. Even when he was a skinny, lanky, awkward, aggravating, pre-puberty pain in my rear, had he looked this bad to me. He started to rise from the couch with a grin finally showing on that gaunt face and I started crying, telling him not to get up. I went to the couch and sat down beside him. We hugged each other as best we could between the plastic and metal I had on and the layers of quilts he had on. We sat there for a long time just holding hands.

Finally, I looked at his face and asked, "How was it?"

He looked down at the floor and said, "It wasn't too bad."

After a while, he tried to poke me in the ribs and hit the plastic and metal brace. "How're you doing with this?" he asked.

I too looked at the floor. Squeezing his hand I said, "It's not too bad. Mama says it'll get well before I get married." We both laughed out loud at another one of Mama's wisdom phrases. Even though we both knew the other was lying, we knew we were going to make it though this part of our lives and that we had each other to rely on. We never passed another harsh word between us except in fun after those days of war and healing. From that day forward, we have always introduced each other to other people by saying, "This is my favorite brother, Glen" or "This is my favorite sister, Belvia."

I had seen Daddy cry many tears of sadness and despair during my childhood over the loss of his sons and the illnesses and traumas the family had faced. He never sought the help of anyone to ease his burdens, but he prayed a lot. He didn't know anyone was watching, but sometimes I would catch him sitting on an old stump in the woods with his elbows on his knees and his forehead resting on his clinched hands. I always knew when he was talking to God, because he would take his hat off and hang it over one of his knees. He had done a lot of praying like this over the last few years with Dennis' death, my surgery and recovery, and Glen's tour of duty. Daddy usually got home around three o'clock in the afternoon, but the day Glen came home, he was very late. He was always punctual so Mama didn't call the post office to let him know Glen was home. She wanted to surprise him. Mama was furious because he had not even called to let her know where he was. About five-thirty, Daddy came strolling in the back door.

"Where in the world have you been?" Mama shouted accusingly.

"I went with Joe up to the lake to help him get his boat out of the water for the winter. What's wrong with that?"

As Daddy came further into the kitchen, Mama said in her high pitched voice of excitement, "Look who's here!" She motioned to the door between the kitchen and dining room, dish towel in hand. There in the doorway stood Glen with his right hand stuck out to shake hands with Daddy.

Daddy looked in Glens face and said, "Well, I'll be," grabbed Glen's hand and jerked him into a big bear hug. I was standing a few feet behind Glen and got to see the sheer relief as tears of joy streamed down Daddy's face. His tears of joy were so much better to see than his shoulders shaking in sobs of despair. I was so happy for my parents on that day. Finally something good had happened to them with one of their children. They were finally getting something out of all that praying Daddy had been doing all those years. Maybe this God that Daddy seemed so close to wasn't such a bad sort after all. I had always felt that I was supposed to fear God and if I didn't do what I was supposed to punishment would surely be in store for me. We had been told in Sunday school all about the Israelites and all the bad things God would do to them when He got angry. I didn't want God sending Charlton Heston down the mountain to throw the Ten Commandment tablets at me. Yet, after Glen came home, I began to fear God less and think He was not as angry as the Old Testament made him out to be with the Israelites. I started praying for God to bring the day when I would get out of this uncomfortable brace and be a normal teenager.

The days passed during that winter with everyone in better spirits because Glen was home. Mama got him to the dentist within a few days of his return and he stopped his aspirin eating binge. He got his belly full on Mama's famous beef roast and gravy, which to this day I cannot duplicate. She made him gravy of some sort every day. There was milk gravy when she fried chicken, beef gravy when she boiled a roast and some other kind of gravy that she made for her country style steak that I cannot duplicate either. In fact, the only gravy that I can make better than my mother's is sausage gravy and that's only because I don't think she ever made it. She always put either biscuits or cornbread on the table every night for dinner and made yeast rolls for

Sunday. She always said, "If you have good bread, sweet iced tea, and strong coffee with a meal, it doesn't matter if anything else you have is good." All the special attention that got channeled toward Glen was great for me. He got to take some of the heat for a while.

The next day I marked on the calendar was the day I was to get to stop wearing my back brace. Six months living with that thing was an eternity for a fourteen year old girl. I had an appointment during the middle of March, 1968. I was praying hard for this ordeal to be over. When Dr. Jones finally said I could take it off forever, I joyously hugged him and presented him with a vest that I had knitted him while I was in my cast the previous summer. "Belvia, I will always treasure this sweater. You and I have been through a lot together in the past two years and I will never forget you. Now, are you going to keep your brace for posterity?"

"Yes sir!" I said emphatically. "I have a special place picked out for it at home." We used to burn our paper trash in a barrel out near the sheds. Down the road to our river bottom pasture there was a ravine that Daddy was trying to fill up. It was in the woods and nobody could see it from the road in front of our house. It was hidden from the house by the trees. That is where we always threw any garbage that we couldn't burn. All the cans Mama had opened were down there, even the old ringer washing machine that Mama had when I was little was there probably turned into the home of some snakes or a skunk. As soon as we got home from Dr. Jones' office, I took the brace in hand and started walking down the driveway.

"Where are you headed with that thing, Bel Henry?" shouted Daddy using the nickname he had always called me by.

"I'm going to the dump." I walked with great resolution and determination toward the river to accomplish my task. I suppose Daddy saw his own stubbornness in his only daughter and said no more. As I hurled the brace, I thanked God for that wonderful day and the ravine received the metal and plastic monstrosity with open arms.

Eighteen years later, I went to work at the hospital where I had my surgery and Dr. Jones was still practicing medicine. One day, much to my surprise he was wearing the sweater I had made.

"Dr. Jones, I can't believe you are still wearing that sweater."

"Sure I am, Belvia. It's the best one I have. Do you still have your brace?"

"Oh, yes sir, I know exactly where it is. It's still down at Mama and Daddy's place." To this day, it is still in that ravine like all the rest of our old garbage, covered up by the vines and wild foliage that being in the woods for years will bring. Maybe thousands of years from now some archeologist will dig it up and try to figure out what it is and why it is there beside the ringer washing machine.

The next morning after getting rid of the brace, I got ready for school. Mama had made me a pretty navy blue dress that was more fitted to my body. It had a white collar with a small cotton lace sewn to the edge. The lace was sewn around the bottom of the sleeve as well. She also had gotten me some hose and a new pair of loafers. As I combed my hair looking in my bedroom mirror, I realized the day I had been praying so hard for was finally here. Mama walked up behind me and smiled at me in the mirror. I turned to her and laid my head on her ample breasts and sobbed saying, "I have prayed so hard for this day to get here." She quickly took my face in her hands, wiped my tears and said, "Oh Bel, you don't pray for things like that. You pray for God's presence in your life and you pray for God to help others who are in need of his help, but you never pray for yourself. Now, dry your eyes and finish getting ready for school. You're going to ride the bus from now on." While I was delighted to hear that I would be riding the bus with the neighbor kids again, my joy in feeling like my prayers had been answered was squashed like a bug.

I did have great fun riding the bus again with the kids that I had missed being with every day. I hadn't told anyone at school that I was going to see the doctor about getting my brace off for fear it wouldn't happen. I walked down to the library before I had to go to homeroom to start my school day. From behind I heard someone shout, "Belvia Holt, turn around!" Pam, a good friend from my hometown, had a huge smile on her face. She ran up to me, hugging me and patting me on the back, telling me how pretty my dress was and how great I looked. After that I was surrounded by all my girlfriends who had been so wonderful to me. We all cried and laughed and hugged each other there in the hall outside of the library.

I know now that I was one fortunate girl to have God send me the support of my family and friends during this whole episode in my young life. My mother devoted her entire life to my care during those months and I am forever indebted to her for it. My friends who gathered around me during this time, I still consider to be the best friends anyone could ever have. And God bless my dear Aunt Bib for being there for me to talk to and allowing me to be a normal teenager in her home. She became my tree branch to sit on and ponder through all the difficult times.

Over the next few years, Glen and I both were becoming unsure of God and the church as the truth of how life was supposed to be lived. Glen had moved back into an apartment close to where he worked and I was at home by myself with my parents again. Glen was getting away from attending our church. He did help with the Methodist Youth Fellowship of which I was a member, but that was about it. After he got back from his military tour in Southeast Asia, he felt there was a lot of hypocrisy going on in the world. He didn't understand how people from the church could be so righteous on Sunday and then on Monday criticize and judge those who had fought for their freedom. I pondered over how much bad had happened to our family over the years. If God was all powerful and could allow all this to happen to two good people like my parents, who really needed Him anyway. Also, if I couldn't pray for this God to help me when I needed it, then my recovery and getting through that awful time with my back would have happened anyway without asking for anybody or anything to help me.

As I neared high school graduation, I was becoming more and more rebellious, wanting nothing more enormously than to get away from home. The overprotection of my parents toward me had continued throughout the remainder of my high school years. I was definitely not going to be allowed to go with any of my friends to Myrtle Beach the week after graduation. I knew before I asked that such a request would be emphatically refused. Rather than tell me I couldn't go to college because they didn't have any money, they wanted me to believe that because my grades had dropped during the eighth and ninth grade while I was dealing with my back issues, I would never get in a college. I graduated lacking only two tenths of a point to graduate with honors. Daddy wanted me to find something to do in medicine. It didn't cost much to go to nursing school and I would always be able to find a job. I really didn't want to be a nurse, so I went to the guidance counselor at school. The only other medical profession I knew much about was x-rays since I had so many in my early teenage years. "Mr. Rowland, could you check out some places for me that I might be able to learn to take x-rays fairly cheaply?" I wanted to become totally independent, taking care of myself and the sooner the better. I had been told that x-ray school only took two years.

Mr. Rowland found two places in the state that my parents would allow me to consider going. One was at a small hospital in Harrisonburg and the other was in the city of Roanoke. Burnette and I applied and were accepted to both schools. Mama and Daddy took us to look at them. The one at Harrisonburg was just a two room x-ray department in a small hospital run by a matronly old nurse who would have watched us like a hawk, making sure we were escorted to our dorm rooms at the college next door and protected from the world at all times. The one in Roanoke was quickly growing into a large hospital. The x-ray department was in a new building with eight rooms and the most up to date equipment available. We could rent rooms from people near there and eat our meals at the hospital. Tuition was free and all that my parents would have to pay for was my uniforms, books, and forty dollars a month for a room rental.

Of course, Daddy wanted me to go to Harrisonburg where that old matron would watch over me. I had other plans. Janet and I talked Daddy into Roanoke by explaining that their facility was bigger and more modern. We would get a better education there. Daddy finally agreed to Roanoke and in July of 1971, Burnette and I were off to begin our education to become Radiologic Technologists. I really didn't want to be a Radiologic Technologist either; I just went there because I felt it was my only avenue to get away from home. Burnette didn't really know what she wanted to do. She just figured she would come with me.

Finally having some much wanted freedom, I turned into a constant fun seeking party animal. This new wild life was exciting and exhilarating. I didn't care much about school; I was too busy wondering everyday who I was going to get to buy the Boones Farm Apple wine that night. I would drink until I either passed out or threw up. I decided to carry on the Holt family tradition and started smoking cigarettes. I eventually was introduced to marijuana which I found much more enjoyable. I could smoke that until I passed out and not get sick or have a hangover the next morning. Using marijuana led to other drug experimentation. I became known as "Little Hippie."

I had turned my back on God, sped away and left him standing in the dust. Looking back on those times, I thought I was on my own and didn't need anybody or God for anything. Fate, luck, karma, kismet, whatever term you prefer was becoming my replacement for faith in God. Of course, I know now that God was with me, protecting me through those times. I was tempting fate at every turn and only God was powerful enough to have saved me from myself. I thank God today that He kept His covenant with me even when I turned away. If He had not, I would not have lived through my early twenties.

I was of the complete mindset that I didn't need God. I wasn't even sure what He was. None of my questions were ever answered in my childhood church life to my satisfaction. My brother had even pulled away from the church and a relationship with God. I just couldn't believe anything except that we controlled our own destiny, life was our choice and would be what we made it. The decisions were ours, good or bad, to live with and die with.

Darkness to Light

Stagnation . . . no movement, no progress, no real life. The water is murky and dark. The few organisms managing to survive there are faded white from lack of sunlight. Trying to surface is near impossible without being covered with slimy mold and rotting vegetation. The air is thick with the odors of decay and bugs in search of warm blooded beasts to feast upon. The albino organisms have no hope of a better future. They are lost to survive in darkness. Yet, eventually a torrential rain will burst forth from the heavens, flooding that stagnant mire and washing it all away. Movement starts anew, freshness appears, and the light shines in the clear waters giving new life and joy where there was none.

There wasn't too much out on the streets in the early 1970's that I didn't get into. I made a lot of bad decisions during that time in my life. I walked away from good relationships and hung tight to bad ones because nobody was going to ever tell me again what I could and could not do. I finally got wise enough to know I needed to get away from some of the bad influences in my new found life of total freedom.

Going home was getting harder and harder to do. Mama was always complaining about Daddy. He just didn't understand how she felt and what she was going through. I didn't understand what she was going through that he hadn't gone through, too. Daddy had always been active in the community, helping get the community center started, working to build a volunteer fire department, teaching the Men's Bible Class at church, visiting his friends, helping wherever he was needed. Mama on the other hand now wanted nothing to do. She had always devoted her life to taking care of us. Her last two children had left the nest; she was on her own. Instead of becoming more socially active herself, she preferred being at home as she always had been and now wanted Daddy to stay home with her. "Your Daddy is gone every night of the week. He needs to stop all his gallivantin' around and stay home with me."

Although it nearly killed him, Daddy did stop many of his extra activities. There was nothing he liked better than laughing and joking with his friends, being with people. Now he went home from work, ate the supper that Mama fixed for him that she had to be done with, having the dishes washed, dried and put away by six o'clock so she could watch the news. His evenings were spent watching television until it was time to go to bed. Daddy was not happy and neither was Mama. As she had done when I was young, Mama still recanted the old stories about her children whenever there was anyone to listen. Daddy was getting his ear full now of what Glen and I had heard all our lives while he was at work or gallivantin' around, as Mama called it. It had gotten to the point I would only go home on Sunday afternoons periodically for short visits.

Daddy had wanted to travel when he retired from work. Mama complained that she had trouble riding in the car for long periods of time. Her stomach was too sensitive and she would have to go to the bathroom too often. Mama had never had trouble traveling before. We had been to Illinois several times. We had been to the beach a lot over the years. We had taken a trip to Canada once. Daddy finally talked

Mama into a trip to Illinois to see his family and then to Colorado to see hers. She agreed to go if I would drive and we made the journey to Illinois in two days rather than making the thirteen hour trip in one day. It was their intention to spend a week in Illinois and then go on to Colorado for a week. I could not get the time off from work for two weeks. Catherine and X, our family in Illinois said they would drive Mama and Daddy to Colorado. I could drive them to Illinois; after a week they would then take me to St. Louis and put me on a plane back to Virginia on their way to Colorado. Daddy would only have to drive back to Virginia from Illinois on the return trip and Mama and Daddy could take as many days as they wanted to get home. Everything sounded like it would be wonderful. It was all planned out. Mama wouldn't have to help Daddy drive at all and they could have a leisurely two week vacation.

The trouble started by the time I had driven fifty miles. Mama started back seat driving. "Just because that sign says 35 miles an hour doesn't mean you have to go 35 miles an hour . . . it is twenty miles to Blacksburg . . . watch for that turn we need to make to get to the turnpike . . . you can go to Virginia Polytechnic Institute and State University from the next three exits . . . welcome to Wild, Wonderful West Virginia." By the time we hit the West Virginia turnpike, Daddy and I were chain smoking cigarettes. Mama read aloud every road sign, bill board, painted barn or the state of any license plate we came to. By the time we got to Louisville, Kentucky, she had plucked my last nerve. I pulled the car off the road.

"Mama, we are getting ready to go through Louisville and I know there are a couple of strategic signs we need to watch for to make the right turns for the bridge that will take us into Indiana. If you want to drive right now, I will be happy to let you take the wheel."

"No Belvia, I don't want to drive. That's what we brought you for."

Restoring Spirit

"Well then, if you want me to drive this car through Louisville, you are going to have to sit back there and be quiet. I don't want to hear another word out of you. Daddy will watch for the turns we need to make and tell me when to make them. If I so much as hear a peep out of you, I will not drive another mile. Do you think you can do that?"

"Yes, I guess I'll have to."

Surprisingly enough, she was quiet for the rest of the trip to Illinois. I could tell she was peeved with me when I would look at her in the rear view mirror. She would turn her face away from me and look out of the window. She was wringing her hands like she always did when she was worried about something, but she was quiet. After we arrived at X and Catherine's house, Mama seemed to calm down some. We had a good visit with the family and the time finally came for me to fly back to Virginia. The closer we got to St Louis, the more Mama started wringing her hands. She was becoming quite distraught. By the time I was to board my flight, she was in tears. "What is wrong, Mama?"

"I just don't want you to leave me. I'm scared of planes and I don't want to see my baby get on one."

"Oh Mama, don't be silly. I'll be fine. I'll be safer in that plane than you will be with X driving to Colorado doing 70 miles an hour. You can call me from Colorado when you get there so we will all know that everybody is alright." Mama's tears faded and we all laughed and hugged and said our goodbyes.

The next time I saw Mama and Daddy was a week later when they drove up in the driveway at my apartment on their return trip. It was about eight-thirty in the evening. I came out of my apartment to welcome them home to find them fussing with each other as they got out of the car.

"Carl Holt, I told you before we went on this trip that I had trouble with my stomach and I would have to stop to go to the bathroom. And you wouldn't stop anywhere to stay the night and made me ride all the way back home in one day. I am sick, Carl. I tell you, I am sick and you won't listen to me."

"Shirley, you made us get up to leave Catherine's by five o'clock this morning. There was no need to stop anywhere to get a room when we should have been home by six o'clock tonight. If you hadn't had to stop every twenty miles to take a shit, we'd have been home a long time ago."

As she headed for my door, Mama brought up both her hands and then quickly threw them down in a huff as if to say, "I have had quite enough of your mouth, Carl Holt." She brushed by me without a word and headed for the bathroom.

Daddy looked at me and shook his head, "Bel, I swear if I'd had a gun, I'd have gone ahead and shot her to put her out of her misery. She has done nothing but gripe and complain ever since we left X and Catherine's."

"Has she been like this ever since I left you in St Louis?"

"No, not at all, she was fine until we got on the road this morning. I tried to tell her last night that we didn't need to leave so early if we were going to stop and spend the night, but she was adamant about leaving Catherine's before the crack of dawn. As soon as we left she started in with the wringing hands and complaining about her stomach. She wanted me to stop and get a room at two o'clock this afternoon. The closer I got to Virginia the more I wanted to just make it home and not drag this into another day of some of the same."

Daddy did finally make it home that night. Mama went to bed and didn't get out of it for a week except to go to the bathroom and get a little something to eat. Daddy called me from the hospital to tell me that he had Dr. Shreve come out to the house to check on Mama and now she was on the psychiatric ward at the hospital. They had a psychiatrist treating her for severe depression, which was then often called a nervous breakdown.

This took us all somewhat by surprise. I knew Mama was not her usual self with this episode of staying in bed all the time. She had never done that unless she was ill, which was rare. Mama had always seemed so strong. She had spent her entire life taking care of others. Now that she had time to make a life for herself, she felt she had no life or had no control over her life. Maybe it was that she had no more control over our lives. Whatever the reason, she did not feel needed anymore. Mama told the psychiatrist that people were always trying to get her to go out and do things that she really didn't want to do like join a club, or play cards, or become more active at church to fill her time. She didn't want to do anything like that. She just wanted to stay home and take care of everything. The psychiatrist kept Mama in the hospital for a couple of weeks, put her on an anti-depressant, and told her she didn't have to do anything she didn't want to do. The doctor had given Mama the permission she felt she needed to take charge of her own life and do for herself instead of others. Unknowingly, he had also given her permission to become inactive. She felt she had worked her fingers to the bone all these years to take care of everything. Now was going to be the time that she could just sit down. She had always been a homebody. Now she would become more hermit-like than she had ever been. That two week vacation was the last trip my parents ever took. I don't think they went any further than fifty or sixty miles from home after that, which suited Mama just fine. She gradually came out of her complaining stage and seemed happier again. Yet she seemed more self-oriented from that time on. Perhaps she had been that way all along, but I had just never noticed it. Maybe she just became more vocal about her wants, her needs, how nobody had ever lived as hard a life as she had, and she felt she deserved more.

It seemed so strange to me the differences I saw in my parents now. Daddy wanted to live his life and enjoy what he'd been given. He loved people, going places, growing vegetables, having animals to take care of just because he loved them. He liked having work to do and staying busy. He liked to laugh and have fun. He would go to town to get a loaf of bread for Mama and run into somebody he knew to talk to and be gone for hours. He did get back into having a garden again. He put it up at the other end of the property across from Margaret and Kyle's house. Kyle was not able to work because of a bad heart and Mama didn't want to work a garden. It was favorable for both families that Daddy and Margaret worked the garden and split the harvest. Mama wanted nothing to do with any kind of work that she didn't have to do. She was now retiring too. She didn't want to have to pull weeds out of a flower bed or take care of any animals that she couldn't put on the table for dinner. And now you could buy all that at the store. I tried to give Daddy a beagle puppy to keep him company and Mama made me take it back because she didn't want to have to take care of it. I know Mama had worked hard all her life. During my childhood, she had raised chickens, sold eggs, milked cows, made butter, canned vegetables, made clothes, cooked and kept house for her family. I guess she deserved the right to sit down if that's what she wanted to do. She often voiced that she had worried and done for everybody else all of her life and it was time she looked out for Shirley.

In the late 1970's, I was staying away from my old pot smoking cronies and had moved on to a new set of friends who still liked to party and have a good time. We kept it legal with alcohol abuse. I remember during this time in my life often feeling that I was missing something. Happiness kept eluding me. Rather than being depressed about my unhappiness, I would drink my blues away. While I never actually became an alcoholic, I was well on my way. I did delve into Transcendental Meditation for a time, looking for something to calm my spirit and show me what this life was all about. The reason I am not going to write much more about my life in the 1970's is because like one of my lifelong friends always says, "I don't remember too much about the 70's." Don Everly of the Everly Brothers once said, "Nothing good ever came out of the 70's." Both of these statements fit my existence during that time. That is all it was, an existence. I really didn't like my life or myself anymore and I really didn't care much about anything. I was sick of living in the shadows of my family's past and listening to Mama talk about her depression. Was there no future with anything else in it?

I do remember walking out of Mama and Daddy's house to leave one Sunday afternoon. Their new minister was standing on the porch with Daddy. I heard Daddy tell him, "I worry that Belvia and Glen have left the church and God. I don't know what to do about it. They are both old enough to decide for themselves."

The minister put his hand on Daddy's shoulder and said, "Carl, sometimes you just have to stop worrying about it and put it in God's hands. God will bring them around in his own time." Daddy just shook his head up and down and looked in the minister's face, shook his hand and thanked him for his wisdom.

Something good did eventually come out of the 70's for me. I met my husband, Richard. When I met Richard in the summer of 1979, I was still a pretty heavy drinker. There were a lot of nights I would drive home and the next morning not remember how I got there or wake up in the car in the driveway. I really didn't tone my drinking down much while Richard and I were dating, but he only saw me on the weekends so I had the rest of the week to do as I always had.

Over the years I had become a cynic about my relationships with men, feeling that no one was going to look after me but myself. I really didn't need anyone else to survive. I could take care of myself. God had become some unknown power out there in the universe that I knew was greater than me, but I didn't understand why my parents, especially Daddy, had always thought this God thing was so great; I didn't care to understand. This power could be Daddy's God if he needed Him, but I was self-sufficient and intended to remain so.

After dating Richard for two years, I decided that if I wanted a home and family I had better get at it. I wasn't getting any younger. I let Richard know that he could either join me in that endeavor or I would be moving on. Romantic ultimatum, don't you think? Richard and I were married on October 3, 1981 in the home he had been working on remodeling for several years. I was twenty-eight years old and he was thirty one. Richard was becoming the stability in my life that I greatly needed but would never admit. I did stop drinking as much as I had been. Every week or so I would go out one night with my girlfriends and have a few too many, but it was no longer an every night deal like it had been. Yet, I did still enjoy indulging in the night life I had enjoyed when I was single and wanted to engage in that whenever I felt like it. I wasn't going to let anything, like a husband, change that. I'd had quite enough of people controlling my life when I was young. I wasn't going back to that now.

Before we were married, I had already started spending more of my evenings doing knitting and needlework. I had also started doing some photography before Richard and I met. I had a black and white photographic enlarger and Richard built me a darkroom with a sink and running water in it at the end of the garage. I had been doing some wedding photography on the side and also would make black and white negatives of old photographs and reprint them for people.

I learned photo coloring as well. I got frustrated with how things were going at work, so I came home one day and told Richard I had resigned my full time job. I figured we could make it on his salary for a while and I would look for something else to do. I kept doing my photography work and started a small business called "The Shutter Release" that I ran from home. We were making it, but money was pretty tight. Eventually, I got a part time job at a satellite emergency center that the hospital I had worked for opened. One week I worked evenings for three 8 hour shifts. The next week I worked Saturday and Sunday, twelve hours both days. This job was great. I had a regular pay check coming in to help with the bills and I could still do my photography work on the side.

We would go to church sometimes where Richard's parents went and Richard had grown up. I was quite reluctant about going, but went along with it. I refused to participate in any special activities that would commit me to any extra time at the church and never moved my membership from the Methodist church back home.

I became pregnant sometime in March 1983. The doctor set my due date at November 28. Daddy had been retired for several years and was really starting to have problems from his life long bout with high blood pressure. He started having mini-strokes that were slowly but surely taking their tole on him. I remember the day we told him I was pregnant. "Are you ready to be a grandfather, Daddy?" I asked him with my family and Richard's all sitting on our patio. Glen had married his wife, Nita, only about a year before Richard and I were married. This child I was going to give birth to would become my parents' first and only grandchild.

Daddy grinned at me and said, "Yeah Bel Henry, I think I'm about ready now." My parents had been made to wait until their youngest child was thirty years old to get the chance to become grandparents.

At the time I shared my news with them, Daddy was seventy-one years old and Mama was sixty-five. The more pregnant I became, the weaker Daddy got. I often wondered if he would still be with us when this child was born. Mama was in her element again. Daddy needed her to look after him. She was always happiest when she had someone to care for. My pregnancy went along without a hitch. I didn't get sick unless I did something too strenuous or got too hot. I kept on working my part time night shift job and started taking several different types of craft classes while I was pregnant. I took classes in macramé, watercolor, tin punch, cut and pierced lamp shades, stenciling, and folk art painting. I wanted to stay home with our baby when it came, so I intended to turn "The Shutter Release" into not only a photography business, but a craft business as well. There were a lot of craft shops popping up everywhere and many people were selling their art at craft shows all around the state. I was gearing up to continue my self-sufficiency and stay home with our baby at the same time. Hopefully at some point I would be able to do that. I remember walking back from the neighbors house one day in August and checking my cantaloupes that were planted in front of the dog lot. I must have stepped on the edge of the patch where the grass started. The next thing I knew, I was on the ground, on my right side. I laid there for a few minutes holding my stomach, fearing that something would happen to the baby. After a few minutes, I wasn't feeling anything out of the ordinary, so I got up and went to the house and didn't think anymore about it.

    I left home for work on Thursday, October 13, 1983. I was seven and a half months pregnant and still feeling really good. I stopped at a market near work. I wanted some Krispy Kreme donuts. While I was in the store, a torrential rain storm started. It was raining in buckets full when I came out of the store. I tried to walk really fast to the car, holding my stomach so as not to hurt the baby. I had the key to let everybody in at work and didn't want to be late. I took a few of those steps to the car in a jog. We were busy at work that night. I finally got to sit down about ten o'clock and proceeded to eat a half-dozen of those yummy donuts I had been craving since that afternoon. I got off from work at eleven and decided to go to the grocery store for a few things before I went home. I liked going to the store at that hour because there was nobody there and you could get what you wanted and get out with no hassle. I got home about midnight and put the groceries away, got ready for bed, and lay down beside Richard who was always asleep at this late hour. As soon as I lay down my water broke. I jumped up and ran to the bathroom as fast as I could and sat on the toilet. How could this be happening now? I was not due for another six weeks. We hadn't even finished Lamaze classes yet. We didn't have the nursery ready and I didn't even have a bag packed to go to the hospital.

"Richard" . . . silence . . . "Richard" . . . more silence . . . "RICHARD!!"

"WHAT?"

"MY WATER HAS BROKEN!!"

"Are you sure?"

"AM I SURE? HELL YES I'M SURE!! GET UP!!"

By the time I had gotten off the toilet, called the hospital and thrown a few things in a suitcase it was one o'clock in the morning before we got to the hospital. I had started having contractions in the car and by the time we got there I was pretty uncomfortable. Everything started happening fast. I was hurting badly and more quickly than expected. My contractions were hardly ever letting up. I had wanted to have a natural child birth. I did not want anybody sticking any big needles in my spine after I had so much trouble with it when I was young. Right now all I wanted was some good drugs to make this pain go away. Of course, I could have none. It seemed like these constant contractions would never end. After about three hours that seemed like days, the nurses called Dr. Pasley, my obstetrician. The baby's heart rate was starting to drop some and they were concerned. Just before he got there, my contractions stopped and I felt the uncontrollable urge to push. When that happened, blood gushed from me into the bed. The nurses were yelling at me, "Don't push. Don't push." I couldn't help myself. There was nothing I could do to stop it.

The baby's heart rate starting dropping fast then and Dr. Pasley walked into the room. He took one look at what was happening and asked how much I had dilated. One of the nurses told him it was only two centimeters. I needed to be at ten centimeters for this baby to be born now. "Get this woman ready for the OR. We are going to have to try to do an emergency C-Section and I'm not sure the baby will make it until we can get her to the OR." I tried to keep calm. All I could think was that this child could not die before Daddy saw it. The nurses were hurrying as fast as they could to get me ready for surgery. After what I have always thought was about twenty or thirty minutes, they were getting ready to push me to the OR when I told them I had to push again. "No way, let's go," said one of the nurses.

"No, I'm telling you I really have to push and I don't think I can stop it." Dr. Pasley heard me and stopped them to check me again.

"She has dilated to ten. Get her in the delivery room next door and I'll take the baby with the forceps." I remember being rolled into that room and Dr. Pasley telling Richard to wait outside when he tried to follow. Dr. Pasley introduced me to the anesthesiologist and he said he was going to put me to sleep now. As the mask went over my face and the anesthesiologist told me to take some deep breaths, I saw a team of people getting ready to resuscitate the baby and Dr. Pasley, forceps in hand, waiting anxiously for the anesthesiologist to give the go ahead that I was asleep.

I woke up back in the labor room that I had just been moved from. Dr. Pasley came in telling Richard and me we had a three and a half pound baby girl that was being put in an incubator in the nursery. They were going to check her out and watch her closely, but from the way she had screamed when they tried to resuscitate her, her lungs were in good shape and they expected her to be alright. I had gotten to the hospital at 1:00 AM on October 14, 1983 and our baby girl was born at 5:30 AM. I wanted to know what had happened to make this birth premature. Dr. Pasley said that they usually didn't know why it happened, but my placenta had torn and it was a good thing that I had dilated as fast as I did so he could pull the baby out with the forceps before she bled to death. She never would have survived the time it took to get to surgery. I told the doctor about the fall I had in August and what had happened the day before when I ran to my car in the rain, wondering if either of those things caused it. He said, "We'll never know, but don't worry about it. Just be thankful that your girl is alive. I want you to go to a room they have waiting for you and rest. We'll get you up about seven o'clock tonight and let you go see the baby. I don't want you out of bed until then."

Before the nurses took me to my room, one of them asked me what I was going to name my baby girl. I had always known I wanted to name a boy Peyton Holt. Peyton was the name of one of Daddy's cousins. I had always loved his name. I had chosen Holt because it was my maiden name. Richard was pretty agreeable and was satisfied to let me name the baby. I really hadn't decided on any names for girls. I had toyed with the name Kemper from one of my cousins named Kemper Elizabeth who had been named after one of her uncles and our Grandma Holt. I also had a cousin named Cara that I thought would be good. I also liked the name Loren. I didn't like the female spelling of Lauren. I liked the way the name Loren looked when it was written. I had tried putting some of these names with others that might sound right. When the nurse asked me what the name was that I had chosen, the combination I wanted was clear as day. Loren Kemper Tate would be her name. Both nurses in the room chimed at the same time, "Lauren!! There are now going to be seven Laurens in the nursery."

"No there won't. There will be six," I said. "My girl is going to be Loren, L-O-R-E-N." I suppose I could have just gone ahead and named her Peyton Holt. I had given her a boys name anyway. Richard said later that she was going to be spelling that name for people the rest of her life. "That will be OK. I have had to spell Belvia all my life and it hasn't killed me yet."

Richard had gone home to shower, change clothes, and call our parents to tell them the news of Loren's birth. He had just returned when Dr. Pasley came in. Dr. Pasley looked at me smiling and shook his head. I said, "We were pretty lucky in there this morning, weren't we?" I'll never forget what he said to us as he stood there at the foot of the hospital bed.

"I am a Christian. I believe God was looking out for you two and this baby, because there is nothing that happened with the events of her birth that logically or medically should have happened. I have seen a lot of births in my career, but I have never seen a woman's cervix dilate as fast as yours did this morning. Had that not occurred, your daughter would not be alive right now." I knew that he was speaking of a miracle. Well, if God, in whom Dr. Pasley and Daddy believed, had anything to do with our baby being born, I was glad of it. At least, Daddy would get to see his first grandchild before he met his Maker. Deep down, I knew I was experiencing one of the miracles of life.

By about three o'clock that afternoon, I was telling the nurse taking care of me that if she didn't get me a wheel chair and take me down to the nursery to see Loren, I was going to get up and walk down there. She started going on about having to call the doctor to get it OK'd with him. I told her, "You've got fifteen minutes. If you're not back in here with a wheel chair, I'll wave at you as I pass the desk." The nurse did come with the wheel chair before the fifteen minutes was up and I got to hold Loren for the first time ten hours after her birth. She was so tiny. Her head wasn't as big as a tennis ball and was still misshapen from her bout with the forceps. Dr. Grayson, my family doctor who was going to take care of Loren told me, "She probably had quite a headache." As tiny as she was, she still had all her fingers and toes. The nurses said everything had checked out fine so far. Her lungs were fully developed and she may have to stay in the incubator a few weeks until she gained some weight. One of the nurses said, "She looks just like her Daddy." Richard said, "Ain't she purr-dy!"

Mama did come the fifty plus miles to the hospital to get a look at her first born grandchild the day she was born. She got Daddy's sister, Bib, to come to the house to stay with him while she came to see us that day. Daddy had been getting weaker and weaker. Mama was having a harder and harder time taking care of him. He had been in and out of the hospital several times. She couldn't leave him by himself anymore. She came bustling into my room all flustered that the baby had been born too early. We assured her that all was well. Loren was going to be fine; she was just going to have some catching up to do in the size department. Richard's mother, Becky, was already there and took Mama down to the nursery to see Loren. Mama came back beaming, cupping her hands together in front of her. "She ain't no bigger than a squirrel!" She was satisfied now that everything would be alright and headed back home to look after Daddy.

I went home from the hospital after three days. Loren had to stay in the incubator for two more weeks. At that time they usually kept premature infants until they weighed five pound. Loren had done so well and had so few medical problems that we were able to bring her home early at four pounds.

I pondered a lot about what Dr. Pasley had said about God looking out for us. I knew I had been given a beautiful child to love. I intended to make her childhood so much better than mine had been. She would be nurtured and loved, made to feel she could accomplish anything if she set her mind to it, and be taught to make her own decisions. She would be given the chance to make some mistakes at home while she was under my roof and supervision so that she would be prepared for the world when it was her time to go out into it alone. I would be able to use my past experiences to guide her. "Just do what your Mama says" would not be part of my repertoire of answers for her. I made another friend in my 20's, Shirley, whose mother, Emma, was the perfect role model of motherhood for me. When her girls became old enough to start learning to make decisions, Emma would not tell them, "No, you cannot do that." She would advise them of the pros and cons of their decision and tell them what she preferred they would do. The decision making was then left up to them. Nine times out of ten, Shirley told me the girls would do what Emma preferred. Emma never interceded unless it was something they could really get hurt by. The girls learned to deal with the errors of their decisions because Emma had allowed them to make some mistakes and deal with the consequences. I also wanted to keep communication open with Loren. I intended to be very vocal when needed, but wanted to talk things out with her rather than getting angry or dictating. I felt that friendship fostered with a child could be very beneficial for both parent and child. I wanted to have a special relationship with this child that we both could enjoy and remember with fondness. I didn't want to bring this child into the world to have to live in the shadow of her families' sorrows.

I was thirty years old. It was time I started making my own life good and stop blaming my parents for my problems. Life was going to be what I made it, not what my parents had lived in the past. It was time to grow up and get out from under that shadow of sadness. My life was going to change for the better with the birth of this beautiful little child. I just knew it. She was to become the bright light in my life.

Yelling at God

The progression of the James River winding through the Blue Ridge Mountains is a joy to experience in a canoe on a balmy summer day. Sections of the river are slow and lazy meanderings through quiet waters. Oars come up to allow for basking in the sun as the water gingerly carries the canoe downstream. Then suddenly white water rapids appear as the river makes its descent down the mountains and through the valleys. Obstacles unexpectedly appear to thwart the way. Big boulders protrude from the water. Others are unseen just beneath the surface as they reach up to grab the canoe and throw it over and away from its intended path. The water rushes faster and faster as it makes its descent, leaving those having enjoyed their journey until now, frightened by the strength of the stream and their own lack of ability to control it.

These waters are most frightening in late fall after a big rain. The river is swollen with more water, traveling faster and faster. The slow areas are too fast for lazy meditations. The river is king now. The canoe flips into the air as an unseen bolder points it toward the heavens; screams of fear rise up as the cold rushing water envelops the body. A thrashing struggle ensues to fight wet flannel shirts, blue jeans, boots, and the frigid rapids to surface for air. Is it time to die? Perhaps today . . .

Restoring Spirit

The rushing stream finally crashes over a bolder, shooting the body into a deep, wide expanse of water like a child sliding down a big sliding board into a swimming pool. Calmness does return while crawling to the bank, kissing the earth, having made promises to God that He knows won't be kept.

During my pregnancy, Daddy was becoming progressively worse very quickly. Mama did bring him to the hospital once to see Loren. He had a hard time walking into the hospital and once he got to the nursery he was completely worn out. One of the nurses got him a wheelchair to get back to the car. He told Mama on the way home that he wouldn't be able to go see Loren anymore. "Belvia's going to have to bring her to me from now on," he said. After Loren came home from the hospital, I took her to my parent's home as often as I could. Daddy had always loved little children so much. They had always been drawn to him like a magnet. I had so wanted him to have his own grandchild to enjoy. But that was not to be. By the time of Loren's birth he could only hold her for a short time. He would smile and laugh with her, but after a few minutes was ready for me to take her. After he saw Loren for the first time, it was like he had accomplished living long enough to see his grandchild born. That was all he had left to do in life. He became worse quickly and was suffering. He looked up from his bed one day at Mama saying, "Shirley, this is awful. I can't live and I can't die." All he wanted now was to be at peace and be with the God he loved so much.

Mama called me on February 8, 1984 to tell me that the county nurse had been by to check Daddy and said he had gone into congestive heart failure. I knew Daddy had decided long ago that he didn't want to be treated anymore to prolong his life and that it would not be long now. I told Mama I would be down for the weekend and spend Saturday and Sunday with her and Daddy. I had to call Mama on Friday, February 10 to tell her that Loren and I had caught really bad colds. I needed to keep Loren at home for a few days before bringing her out.

"Mama, I'll be off from work again on Tuesday and Wednesday next week and will come down then."

She said sadly, "OK, don't wait too long, Bel."

I called Mama every day to check on Daddy. The news was never good. He was suffering a great deal, gasping for every breath. After calling home on Monday, February 13, I had to get in the shower and get ready to go to work. The more I thought about Daddy's suffering now and throughout his life, the angrier I became. While standing in the shower, with the hot water pelting me, tears streaming down my face and with the wash cloth clutched to my chest, I started screaming at God, "What kind of a God are you anyway? My daddy, this man who has always put You first in his life, has always trusted in You even when things were going badly, has always praised You and told me what a loving God you are, is being made to suffer . . . again . . . in this life. Haven't you done enough to Daddy? You've taken three of his children from him and gave him numerous trials with the other two. Yet, he has always been there for You. Where are You now that he needs You . . . . You, who are supposed to be such a loving, caring, and giving God? Where are You now when Daddy needs Your mercy? You either need to heal him so he can live his life or take him to Heaven so he can be with his boys. You need to stop torturing this man who has always been Your faithful servant and show some compassion."

When I got home from work around 11:30 PM, I had this feeling that I should pack up my things and go home to be with Daddy right then. Had I not had Loren to think about, I would have thrown my jeans and a sweatshirt in the car and been gone. But now, that would mean I would have to pack for myself and Loren, wake her up to get her into the car, and drive an hour and a half in the middle of the night down country roads to get there. Loren and I still had colds but we were both on the mend. I finally decided it wouldn't be a good idea for me to go in the middle of the night with a baby in tow. What if something happened to the car? I'd have to be walking in the cold with a sick baby in the dark to a stranger's house for help . . . not such a good idea. Instead, I went to bed. I planned to get up early in the morning and be by Daddy's side by eight o'clock. That would be better. At least it would be daylight and Loren wouldn't be cranky the next day because I had ripped her out of bed in the middle of the night.

It was about 3:00 AM on February 14 when we were awakened by the telephone ringing. I knew without answering that Daddy was gone. Richard answered the phone and handed it to me. I could hear Mama trying to get her composure enough to tell me Daddy was dead. I did it for her. "Mama, Daddy is gone, isn't he?"

"Yes," she finally got the word out through her sobs.

"I'll be home as soon as I can."

"Don't rush, it's too late now."

I had a lot of mixed emotions going on about the chain of events leading up to Daddy's death. Whether intentional or not, Mama always made me feel guilty if I didn't measure up to what she thought I should be. Her statement on the phone made me feel that I should have listened to that gut feeling I had when I got off from work and run to be at Daddy's side. Little did she know that I had yelled at Daddy's God to get off His laurels and do something about Daddy to stop his suffering the very afternoon before he died. I suppose that I should have felt that God did answer prayer in releasing Daddy from his slow suffering death. But I hadn't prayed, I had shouted in anger. I felt that it was about time that Daddy's God woke up and listened to some good reasoning to stop torturing this good man. I also thought about Mama telling me when I was little to be careful what I wished for. It might come true. I had wished for God to either let Daddy get better and live his life or to go on and take him. I knew Daddy would not ever be physically able to live a normal life again and that the best alternative for him was death. Yet, it was still hard dealing with the fact that I had wished for the end of Daddy's suffering and he had died that same night.

    I wrestled with these feelings a great deal. In the spring after Daddy's death, I had gone to church with Richard. There was a guest minister speaking about opening up and allowing God to come into your life. He talked about Jesus dying on the cross so that we might live eternally. He talked of the trinity of the Christian God, Father, Son, and Holy Spirit. All these words I had heard over and over in my childhood. The minister reminded me of the preachers I heard at revivals when I was a child and how Daddy used to always go to the altar. At the end of the sermon, the congregation stood to sing the hymn *Just As I Am,* but before we started singing the minister invited anyone who felt led to give their life over to Christ to come forward, confess their sins, and ask God to come into their life. As we started singing people started going forward, standing arm in arm and hugging each other. I could tell they were crying tears of joy because there were smiles on their faces as well as the tears. The more we sang of this hymn, the more I was reminded of all those times Daddy had gone to the altar to turn his life over into God's hands. I was mourning the loss of my father, one of the most stable forces in my life. I was crying in grief standing next to my husband there in the pew holding my tiny six month old baby that Daddy would not get to love and enjoy. Hearing the music and lyrics of that old hymn that had always been sung as the last hymn of every revival meeting I had ever been to, I felt the flood of the rushing waters of God's love enter my being. God was saying to me, "Belvia, I am here for you. Let me give you my gift of peace. Accept my gift to you." I have heard someone say that when you feel the Holy Spirit enter your body, that you can't help but accept it. I don't believe that statement to be true because God gave us freewill to choose His way or not. I also don't believe it to be true because I balked right there in that church when the Holy Spirit came to me. There was no way that I was going to get involved with this God my own father had faithfully worshipped and served only to be tortured throughout his life with the loss of one child after another and then made to suffer until death finally came. I couldn't wait to get out of that church. When it came time to leave, tears were streaming down my face. Richard looked at me and asked, "What's the matter with you?"

"Nothing," I said trying to wipe the tears from my face with the back of my hand. "I was just reminded of Daddy and started crying." I walked out of that church clutching tightly the baby in my arms with my own voice screaming in my head, "I don't need you, God. Get away from me."

Just as it always does after a death, life goes on. Yet, life was not the same without Daddy. Going home to see Mama was so depressing. The house I had grown up in had always seemed to be so full of life. Even with all the hard times our family had been through, we had kept on living. Not this time. It was like all the life went out of that house when Daddy died, like he rolled it all up and took it with him. The house seemed like a tomb to me, silent and cold. The only way to escape it was to go outside, maybe walk to the river. The fond memories of Daddy were there in the old pastures where Daddy had worked and raised cows and grown corn. I could hear his laughter there. But the house was too full of Mama's mourning that had already gone on and on for years and years and years. Newly fueled by Daddy's passing, it was suffocating.

While Daddy was still living, we had celebrated Loren's first Christmas at our home. Loren had actually had a bilateral inguinal hernia repair on December 23 which we never told Daddy about so he wouldn't worry. She was fine the next day like nothing had happened, but we needed to keep her at home for a few days. Christmas came and went with Loren fine and Daddy not motivating very well; but we were all together, Richard's family and mine. I knew after Daddy's death that going to Mama's for Christmas would be unbearable. Therefore, I decided to make the new tradition for both our families to come to our house for the holidays. I had no intention for my child's Christmases to be overshadowed with sadness and mourning like mine had always been. I wanted a full house with lots of joy and laughter. Christmas was supposed to be a celebration, wasn't it? So let's celebrate!

I really tried to go home less after Daddy was gone. It never became any easier for me to go in that house without him there. We would invite Mama to come up to spend time with us at our home so she could spend time with Loren. Getting her away from that atmosphere of sadness made me feel better at least. Her neighbors were always good to check on her to make sure all was well. She fell in the spring after Daddy's death. Luckily, the nearest neighbor, not in sight of the house, heard her hollering and came to check on her. He found her on the ground in the back yard near one of the sheds. She appeared to have a broken arm.

After her trip by ambulance to the emergency room, Glen and I met her at the hospital. I took her home that night and drove her back to see an orthopedic surgeon the next day to get her dislocated elbow set. I then packed her up and took her home with me until she felt better and could do for herself again. She seemed to enjoy her time with us. She got to spend every waking moment with her granddaughter. Helping take care of the baby gave her purpose and made her happy, something I had not seen in her since Daddy's death.

Mama went home in a couple of weeks and started getting settled into her own life. As long as I can remember, Mama always had a schedule to get everything done by. Rarely did it ever vary. Everything had its time to be done and its place to belong. Monday was wash day, Tuesday was ironing (Mama ironed everything from the dish towels to Daddy's boxer shorts), Wednesday the beds had to be stripped and remade with the sheets and pillowcases she had ironed the day before. On Thursday she spent all day doing her sewing or needlework and Friday was the day to dust and clean the house with a trip to the grocery store in the late afternoon before supper. Saturday had always been the day to get ready for Sunday. Mama had always cooked on Saturday. The majority of our lives when I was a child, people had either come to our house on Sunday to visit and eat or the family would go to Lynchburg to see Dennis. Mama spent Saturdays baking a cake or a pie. She would cook butterbeans and corn and put a roast in the pressure cooker. After church on Sunday, she would heat everything up, make the gravy and biscuits and have lunch on the table by one o'clock.

She kept to a daily schedule after she was on her own with few variations in her routine . . . breakfast at six-thirty, watch the Today Show, read the paper, do her daily chores, watch The Price is Right. Her neighbor, Earnest, always picked up the garbage to take to the dump for her on a certain day and time. She was always ready and waiting at the door to give it to him when he came by. Lunch was always at noon sharp while she watched the 12 o'clock news. Mama swore she never watched the Soap Operas, but the television was always on any afternoon I ever happened to walk in. Her favorites were *As the World Turns* and *The Young and the Restless*. Virginia, Earnest's wife, always called her after her Soaps were off to be sure she was alright. Dinner was at five o'clock with dishes washed, dried and put away by the time for the six o'clock news to come on television. Then it was *Jeopardy* and whatever show she liked to watch in the evening. If there was nothing on TV she liked, she would read the Reader's Digest. She never liked reading books or novels. She wanted to read a story that she could finish in one sitting and be done with. Reader's Digest and her Sunday school lesson were her favorite reading materials. Nine o'clock was bed time, TV off, lights out. It was a major event to interrupt her schedule. Doctor's appointments could not be made in the morning because she had to get her morning ritual done. It was like she thought there was not another bathroom in the entire world. "I just don't feel good in the morning until I get all my morning things out of the way."

For me there was no time to mourn Daddy's death. Loren was still so small; Mama demanded more attention. I did stay home with Loren for a time after Daddy died and worked at my craft business and did babysitting for some friends. I eventually went back to work at the same part time job I had worked when Loren was born. Life was pushing ahead. Privately, I mourned my father's loss tremendously. Because I had turned away from God and the church, I had always viewed my father as the solid foundation of my life. At the time, I didn't realize it was because of his ever present faith in God that I found him to be my stability. It was the living God that I saw in my father's eyes and heard in his voice that made him so special to me. I knew I would never allow myself to have the faith my father did in a God who was so unexplained and invisible and could be so uncaring to one of His most faithful followers. Life moved forward through the mid 1980's. On Daddy's farm, the big oak trees still formed the canopy of shade above the house I grew up in. Storms still brought the sound of rain peppering the tin roof above my old bedroom window. Glen's dog still liked to chase butterflies in the river bottom pasture grass and then jump in the river to cool off. Many things never changed, but the emptiness left by Daddy's death made everything about that place different.

Even though Richard and I eventually built a house on the upper part of the old farm and lived there for ten years after Daddy's death, it was never home to me again. I felt that home was where Daddy had been and he definitely wasn't there now. I did not really want to be there. Mama thrived on the addition to her routine, which was keeping Loren while I worked full time and Richard started a contracting business. Mama was doing fairly well and seemed content having Loren under her wing all the time. Mama had found she was diabetic shortly before Daddy started getting sick. She had kept it in check with diet and medication. She was not insulin dependant and her doctor felt she never would be. But she did always have trouble getting urinary tract infections after becoming diabetic. Not long after we moved back home, Mama started having more and more trouble keeping her sugar down and kept getting more and more infections. It was decided she had to be put on insulin. She went to the hospital for a week, received all the education she needed to give herself insulin shots everyday and went home with her sugar regulated. Glen and I had met with the nurse educator to become more familiar with what we would need to do in the event we found her unconscious. The nurse laughed it off and told us Mama was never going to have that problem. Her diabetes was not that bad that she would ever have any of those kinds of problems. Mama actually surprised us all and did very well with the situation. She had required a lot of attention from all of us after Daddy died. Now with Loren to take care of and her diabetes to keep her the center of attention, she seemed well satisfied with her new life. She became more and more the hermit, only going out to buy groceries or go to church on Sunday. She had a purpose for living now with Loren needing her to be home to put her on the bus for school and to be there when school was over. Glen and I always thought that Mama would have given up, going into some spiraling depression and try to die when Daddy did. She was lost without him in her life. She never missed an opportunity to tell us how much she missed him and her boys who had gone before him. But she found herself a nice little nesting place with Loren in her life and her diabetes to keep Glen and me attentive.

Mama was always harping on me to go to church. "Loren needs to be brought up with God. She'll turn out to be nothing but a little heathen if she doesn't go to church." Thus, whenever Loren misbehaved when she was little, I called her the "heathen child" much to her grandmother's chagrin. "Don't call that child a heathen. What will become of her?" We did go to church some. If we didn't go, Loren always went with Mama. But as she got a little older, she really didn't want to go either and I didn't want to push something down her throat that I actually wanted no part of. Our church going became very sporadic during that time.

Richard had eventually gone to work for a friend of his who had a tile installation business in Salem and then later went back to work for the company he had worked for when we got married. He was driving 90 minutes to work everyday and 90 minutes back. I had been driving 45 minutes to work each way ever since we had moved back to the family farm. The traveling was getting old, yet neither Richard nor I wanted to live back in a city. Richard and I had started looking at houses in the Bedford area. A move to this area would cut Richard's drive to work in half and leave mine about the same. We had been looking for a year. I felt that eventually Mama was not going to be able to live by herself. She had been walking with a walker for quite some time now. I hoped we could find a place that would accommodate Mama and us. She wouldn't have to worry about taking care of that land anymore. She would still be with Loren. I presented the idea to her one day when I went to pick up Loren after work.

She did not like the idea much, but gradually warmed up to it. We told her she didn't have to go with us now. She could stay right there at home if she wanted. Then if the time ever came that she couldn't be alone, we would have a place for her. Loren was reaching the end of her elementary school years. If we were going to move, now would be the time so that Loren could start middle school with a new group of kids that she would get to know before she got to high school. Mama didn't want to leave home, but didn't want to lose having Loren around on a daily basis either. She didn't want anything to change. She decided just not to think about it. "I'll just cross that bridge when I come to it." Anytime our moving was mentioned again, she just threw her hands up as if to dismiss it. She was not going to talk about it. Richard and I kept looking at houses and Mama ignored that anything was going on. It was 1995.

I got a phone call from Mama one day in September, "Belvia, I don't feel very good. I think I've got the flu. Can you get Barbara to keep Loren for a couple of days?"

"Sure Mama, that won't be any problem." Barbara had become a close friend who lived across the road from us and it would be easy for Loren to get on and off the bus there until Mama felt better. "Mama, you give your doctor a call and make sure everything is alright with your diet and insulin if you are sick."

"OK, I will." Two days passed and Mama was not improving. She called me again just before time to go to bed. "Bel, will you come down here and stay with me tomorrow. I've been nauseated all day and I'm just a little weak and need somebody to help me a little until I feel better." I took the next day off from work and went to Mama's the next morning, putting Loren on the bus to go to school from there and telling her to get off there in the afternoon instead of going to Barbara's. Mama was up and around but not herself. I tried to get her to let me take her to the doctor. "No, I'll be fine in a couple of days; it's just the flu."

"What about your insulin? You are not eating like you are supposed to."

"Oh that's alright. I'm not eating because I'm sick on my stomach, so my sugar is not going up. I haven't needed to take any insulin."

I was not very comfortable about how this was progressing, but Mama would have none of my taking her to the doctor. I heard what Daddy had always told me, "Just do what your Mama says." I did make a phone call to her doctor and told him about her not eating or taking any insulin and being nauseated all the time. He called in a prescription for Phenergan to the drug store for Mama to use to settle her stomach. He would see her in the office tomorrow. I had been checking Mama's sugar all day. She had taught me a long time ago how to use her glucometer. I told the doctor that her sugar readings were staying constant at 50, which I knew was low.

"Is she awake?" he asked.

"Yes sir, she is."

"Have her at my office at nine o'clock in the morning."

I called Glen to let him know what was going on and he said he would come down in the morning and help me take Mama to the doctor. Mama and I spent the rest of the day and evening up and down going to and from the bathroom. I was trying to get her to drink fluids which would make her more nauseated. The thought crossed my

Restoring Spirit

mind that maybe she had a urinary tract infection again. She swore to me that she was voiding when she went to the bathroom; it was just the flu. She finally settled down some after midnight. I eventually had talked her into taking her Phenergan dose and she was sleeping. I was exhausted. I felt like I had been fighting a battle with her all day. I lay down across the bed in my old room, thinking I would just rest for a few minutes. I'd get up in a minute and check on her again. After that, maybe I could go to sleep and get up early to get her ready to go to the doctor's office.

I woke up to a big thud. I sat straight up in the bed, not remembering where I was. It finally dawned on me that I was at Mama's and was supposed to check on her again. I must have fallen asleep. It suddenly dawned on me that the thud that had woken me up was probably Mama falling out of bed.

"Mama? Mama, are you OK?" I yelled as I ran across the dining room. I flipped the light on in the bedroom to find Mama in the floor. I frantically tried to wake her up with no luck. She was breathing; I just could not wake her. It must be the Phenergan that knocked her out so badly. She wasn't used to taking any kind of medication like that. It was about five-thirty in the morning. I called Richard.

"Honey, get down here as fast as you can and help me get Mama out of the floor."

"What's going on?"

"I'm not sure, but you and Loren need to come down here as fast as you can to help me."

After they got there it was all Richard and I could do to get her out of the floor and back into bed. She felt clammy. I checked her sugar again. The glucometer reading was still 50, but this time she was not awake.

"Richard, go get some orange juice from the kitchen and let's try to get some down her." She was totally unresponsive and getting her to drink something was not going to happen. I called the rescue squad and then called Glen to meet us at the hospital emergency room. When the rescue squad came, I told Richard to get Loren set up with Barbara to go to school and then he could go on to work. Glen was going to meet us at the hospital and everything would be fine.

Mama's repeated rendition of "It's just the flu" turned into "It's diabetic keto acidosis." She was dehydrated and had a urinary tract infection with a thousand cc's of urine in her bladder. Her blood sugar reading at the hospital was over 800.

I was floored by this information. "I don't understand. Her glucometer reading for the past two days has never been over fifty and she swore to me last night that she was still voiding when she went to the bathroom." The nurse couldn't explain it, but told me that they had a nurse who specialized in diabetic problems and maybe she could help me figure out what had happened. The emergency room called Mama's doctor to get her admitted but the emergency room physician who had been with her was not hopeful that she would live through it. "I have never seen a patient have a blood sugar of 800 and live to tell about it."

All I could think about was hearing Daddy's words, "Do what your Mama says." The thoughts started spinning around my head, "Why on earth did I ever listen to you, Daddy? What was I thinking? I should have stood up to her and you, back then and now. I should have called the rescue squad yesterday whether she wanted me to or not. I knew better. Damn it!"

In the intensive care unit, the nurses hung IV fluid bag after IV fluid bag. There were bottles of antibiotics hooked to those IV's. She had third space fluid shift and became swollen like the Pillsbury

Dough Boy. There were several times that we thought the end was near. Glen bought a new suit and I bought Loren a new dress that she could wear to her grandmother's funeral. That went over like a lead balloon. I worked during the day and then stayed with Mama until bedtime, went home to sleep and came back in the morning. Then one morning when I got to the hospital, Mama was awake.

"Mama, you're here this morning! I'm so glad to see you."

"What is this place?"

"You're in the hospital, Mama. Do you remember being sick at home and not wanting to go to the doctor? Well, you really needed to be in the hospital. We didn't think you were going to make it."

"How did I get here?

"You became unconscious and I had to call the rescue squad to bring you to the hospital." Mama was becoming more and more agitated as this conversation progressed. "It will take you some time to get well again, but we'll take care of you and get you back on your feet."

"Will somebody come and get me out of here," she yelled at the top of her lungs as she tried to sit up, jerking at her IV tubing and nearly pulling the oxygen connector off the wall. The nurses came running. As they tried to get her settled back in bed, she kept screaming, "I don't want to be in the hospital. Take me home. Belvia, I will never forgive you for this." The nurses assured me that the wild behavior that Mama was exhibiting was from the swelling that her brain had done during this ordeal and as the swelling went down, her behavior would improve. It finally became quite obvious after a few days that Mama intended to make a fool out of that young emergency room doctor and live to prove him wrong. She had a blood sugar over 800 and did live to tell about it.

Mama spent a month in the hospital. The diabetic nurse helped me figure out the reason the glucometer only read 50 was because the strips

Mama was using were out of date. Mama did finally confess that when she started getting readings on her glucometer of 50, she quit taking her insulin and started eating ice cream to try to get her sugar back up. In reality she was raising her sugar level higher and higher. This created the flu like symptoms, the eventual urinary tract infection from the high sugar and the downward spiral that nearly took Mama's life.

"It's quite a miracle that your mother has lived through this incident, Mrs. Tate," were the words the nurse said after we figured out what had happened.

"Miracle," I laughed. "You don't know my mother very well. She is just too ornery to die." After the month in the hospital, Mama could no longer walk. She had to be rehabilitated. The doctor's felt she would never be able to live totally alone again. Arrangements would have to be made to either put her in a nursing home or have someone start living with her. At this point, things started falling into place for our family to move to Bedford. We finally found a house that with a little addition to one of the upstairs bedrooms would be able to hold us and Mama. Richard and I put a contract on it and put our house up for sale. Just like it had happened when we moved from Salem, our house sold in a week. The plan was that Loren and I would stay in Mama's house until Loren finished elementary school in June. If Mama got rehabilitated and could come home before we were ready for her in Bedford, she could just come back to her house with us and I'd get someone to come spend the days with her while I worked.

We would be able to move into the home in Bedford in February. Richard could move there then and start the remodeling that needed to be done. Maybe by the time school would be out, we would all be in Bedford. My favorite brother Glen was very supportive during all this time. I would take care of all Mama's physical needs and he would take care of the financial end. Mama was still getting Daddy's retirement check and also had a little nest egg that Daddy had saved to fall back on. Mama's house had been put in our name years ago, so that could be dealt with however we felt necessary.

Things were going well to make this happen. Mama got out of the hospital about the same time we got Richard and all our things moved to Bedford. One of our neighbors started coming to Mama's house during the day and would fix her breakfast and lunch while I was at work. Loren was always home from school by about three-thirty in the afternoon. I would come home and fix dinner and work in the evenings to help get some of Mama's things she wanted to keep packed up to take to Bedford. I would usually go to Bedford on my day off for a while to unpack and work at the new house or sometimes I would go up on Saturday or Sunday for a while. Mama was getting better so that she did not need someone with her all the time. As long as I got her meals ready for her, she could manage during the day alone, but I never left her alone overnight. This move was going better than I had anticipated. I was very excited. Once again, I thought maybe there was something to this miracle thing after all.

Moving Mama

Diving head first into unfamiliar waters can be exciting until you crack your head on the bottom.

    I was hoping for normalcy to return after our move to Bedford was complete. My hopes were often dashed by the needs of others. Loren was not excited at all about this move. She had lived in Hurt since she was three years old and never remembered living in Salem. She and her best friend, Whitney, were very upset about the miles that would be put between them. They had been inseparable since they met in first grade. The two girls were devastated by the entire situation. We parents promised to try to get them together as often as we could. They could take turns spending weekends at each others house. We would do everything we could to make sure their friendship did not fade.

    Although it was a great relief that she had lived through her ordeal with diabetes, the situation with Mama was not wonderful either. She did not want others to tell her what she needed to do any more than I did. I don't suppose the apple fell too far from the tree in that aspect. She was also not used to someone else having a schedule that conflicted with hers. My schedule conflicted with everything. Adjusting to a new way of life was not on her agenda and she balked at every new obstacle. In her mind, she should be able to get back to her normal position of authority and I would have to cater to her wishes. Although she was regaining her strength and could walk with her walker again, she had become very dependant on having a wheelchair when she was in the nursing home for four months of rehabilitation before returning home. Rather than using the furniture to sit on and getting up to walk to another room, she would sit in her wheelchair and roll from place to place, only getting out of the chair if she had to. I suppose being told she could not live alone anymore meant to her that she needed to be waited on constantly. That became what she expected.

Fortunately, we had managed to get our house packed and moved to Bedford before Mama came home from the hospital. Richard started knocking out walls to make a bigger bedroom upstairs for us and we would use the master bedroom downstairs for Mama. I got the bright idea that during the day while we were still in Hurt I would give Mama something to do to occupy her time and help get ready for the last phase of our move to Bedford. She could roll her wheel chair up to the dressers or china cabinet and pack whatever she wanted to keep for the move to Bedford. I got boxes and packing materiel, garbage bags and masking tape. I showed her how to pack her china and crystal. I asked her to pack the things she wanted to keep and we could gradually start taking these boxes to Bedford on the weekends. She could just leave out anything she didn't want and we would have a yard sale one Saturday after the move was finished.

Mama balked here too. "You think you are Miss in charge. I am not able to do all this packing. I am in a wheelchair for heaven's sake. How do you expect me to do all this?"

"Mama, I don't expect you to do it all. I just thought you could help me out some and it would give you something to do during the day when you are alone."

"Well, I can't do it."

"OK, we'll get it done somehow."

With the help of family and friends we did finally get it all done and when the time came for school to be finished for the year, we were ready for the final leg of the move to Bedford. We packed up what was left of Mama's belongings we were taking with us into her Oldsmobile, called Ol' Blue by all of us except Mama, and left for Bedford.

After a year of trial and error, we finally got settled into a structured environment that Mama could tolerate most of the time and I could still manage to get most necessary things accomplished. Loren's first year at the middle school was hard for her, but by the beginning of the second year she seemed to be finding a new set of friends. Whitney would come to Bedford sometimes for the weekend and Loren sometimes would go to Hurt.

It was a busy time for me. I was working long hours at the hospital and taking call shifts. This involved being called out in the middle of the night or on weekends to go to the hospital to help with emergency patients. I had to make sure Mama had three meals prepared every day of the week and had to make arrangements for her care if I wasn't going to be there. Glen was great about this. He would jump in anytime I needed him. Richard too would sometimes take over if I needed to go out of town. Most of my days off and evenings were spent dealing with appointments, getting Mama's meals ready for the next day, trips to the drug store or grocery store, helping Loren with her homework or taking her various places she needed to be. Richard and I rarely got to spend anytime together. We started going out to breakfast every Sunday morning as our get away time. After a year of living in Bedford, we didn't know anybody except our neighbors. It was hard to make friends in a small town, especially when we worked in different ones. At an anniversary party for the Greens, Aunt Bib expressed her concern for me to my friend Jenny, "I know Belvia is doing what she feels she needs to do, but Shirley is going to drive her crazy." How right she was. I was stretched about as far as I could go. It seemed everybody wanted a piece of me. I felt I was cracking. Tears would start and I couldn't stop them. When I spent an entire day off from work upstairs watching television and crying all day, I decided I better do something. I visited the doctor who was helping me take care of Mama. She started treating me for depression with an anti-depressant, which helped me pull myself together to cope with all the ways I felt I was being pulled.

"You need to find a church to go to," Mama kept harping at me. "Your Daddy would be turning over in his grave if he knew his grandchild wasn't being brought up in the church." She was right about that. Daddy had always made us go to church. Maybe that would be a good idea. I was still not really sure that this God and Jesus thing was the truth and the right way to go. Who really knew what religion or if any religion was part of this power that must be out there somewhere in the universe? I did know that Christianity taught goodness, helping others, peace and hope for a better future. Christians were nice people and living by those teachings wasn't such a bad way to live your life. It would also be a way Richard and I could meet people in the community and become a part of it. I discussed it with Richard and we thought maybe sometime in the future we would start shopping around for a church to attend.

Loren had made several new friends at school and was finally becoming more content with living in Bedford. One of her new friends was having a sleep over one Friday night and had invited her to come.

"Mommy, please let me go?"

"Loren, I don't know anything about these people you want to go stay with."

"It will be fine, Mommy. My friend's name is Erin and her father is the preacher at the Presbyterian Church." Loren was so excited she was jumping up and down, clapping her hands together, begging, "Please, Mommy, Please."

"Well, OK," I gave in. "I can meet her parents when I take you over to their house Friday night." Friday night came and I was stuck at work late. Richard took Loren to Erin's for the sleep over and assured me everything was fine. There were girls there whose parents we had met. Loren was not staying overnight with a bunch of strangers and their house was not very far from ours.

Saturday morning after breakfast, I went to Erin's to pick Loren up. I was greeted at the door by a tall man with prematurely graying hair. He pushed his right hand out toward me to shake my hand and spoke with his thick South Carolina accent, "Hi, I'm Joseph. Is one of these wild girls yours?" Girls were scampering all over the house, squealing and laughing. I laughed and accepted his handshake.

"I'm Belvia Tate. The wild Loren Tate is mine."

"Well, come on in. They are having a big ol' time." I entered their home and sat with Joseph and his wife Karen in their living room for a few minutes talking while Loren got her things together. We discovered that our families had moved to Bedford about the same time. They were just getting used to their new environment too. As Joseph helped me gather Loren's things at the door to leave, he asked, "Are ya'll going to church anywhere?"

"Well, no. Actually, my husband and I were recently talking about shopping around for a church."

"We would love to have you join us for worship sometime if you'd like to. We've gotten a new associate pastor who is trying to get a youth group going at our church. Loren would be a welcome addition to the group. And of course, you and Richard would be welcome too."

"That's nice to know," I smiled and chuckled. "We'll think about it and maybe we'll see you one of these Sundays.

"OK, I'm not going to be pushy or anything; just know you're welcome whenever you want to come."

Loren and Erin were gradually becoming closer friends along with this group of girls at school. It was funny how they had banded together. They were calling themselves *The Magnificent Seven*. It was six girls and one boy, whom they had dubbed "Bubba." Erin had asked Loren a couple of times to come to church with her, but Loren was reluctant. I realized that Loren was not going to be interested in going to church unless we were going. I knew my unbelief was becoming her unbelief.

At dinner one night, I told Richard and Loren, "I want to go to church on Sunday. Loren, you can tell Erin we'll be coming to her church." I looked across the table at Mama who had stopped her fork in mid-flight to her open mouth and was gaping at me.

"Mama, do you want to go? I understand that Erin's church has an elevator that we could use to get your wheelchair to the sanctuary."

"Oh no, Bel, that's alright. It's uphill business to get me anywhere. I'll just stay here. You all go ahead and don't worry about me." She was trying really hard not to be excited, but I could tell she was delighted to hear we were going to church.

Church! We probably had not been to church in at least three years. We would all have to try to dig out something to wear. Loren at least would be no problem. She could wear one of the skirts or dresses she wore to school. I had a dress I had bought to go out to dinner one night when I had gone to Washington, DC to an educational conference for work. I could wear that.

"Richard, have you got anything to wear to church Sunday?"

"Yeah, I'll dig something out."

Sunday came and off we went to church, Loren in one of her sweaters and blue jean skirts, I in my little black dress, and Richard in the fifteen year old black wool suit that he had worn when we got married and a pair of brown cowboy boots. I looked at Richard and thought, "What the hell, at least he doesn't have on plaid pants and a striped shirt like his father wears," and got in the car.

This was the start of our church shopping that never got beyond the doors of Bedford Presbyterian Church. Joseph was actually a pretty good speaker, even with that thick South Carolina drawl. I was also interested in the youth group that seemed to be taking off in the right direction. They were doing different things all the time. I felt this was just what Loren needed to stay busy and keep her out of trouble. Erin made an effort every time she saw us at church to come get Loren to sit with her and Katie in the balcony. It took a little time to get Loren into all this, but as we started becoming more active in this church, she did too. They started a Sunday school class for new people in the church to learn more about what it was to be Presbyterian. Richard and I started going to that, which got Loren to go to the class with the kids her age. This in turn got her interested in the other activities that were going on for the youth. Loren became very attached to Bill and Aimee, the associate pastor and his wife. We all got comfortable with this church family. This was going to be great for Loren.

By Christmas time we were regularly attending Bedford Pres. They had a great choir. I had always liked singing and thought I might give the choir a try sometime if my work schedule would allow it. Loren was really getting involved with the youth group and Richard got a new pair of black shoes for Christmas so he wouldn't wear his brown cowboy boots with his black suit anymore.

Loren had been writing stories and poetry ever since she was about eight years old. This was continuing as an outlet for her, a way to express her feelings, a place to go to sort out her fears. The more time she spent with the Buchanans, the Sunday school class and the youth group, the more spiritually evolved she was becoming. I could see it in her writing. I too was feeling my own faith in God return as I watched her blooming in God's care. I wasn't sure I was ready for what I was experiencing, or if God was ready for me. I felt very unworthy to be one of God's children. I had forsaken him for so long but I intended to try to make this work because it was turning Loren into a beautiful person inside.

 I was getting really bogged down with working, taking call, and trying to take care of my family and Mama. I knew something had to give. I couldn't keep on going non-stop from morning until night and then get jerked out of bed in the middle of the night anymore for those emergency cases at the hospital. Mama would get urinary tract infections fairly regularly. It seemed each bout made her a little weaker than she was before, yet it was very gradual. Pain was a constant nagging force for me now as well. My back was feeling the strain of wearing lead for so long and having to often give Mama assistance getting up and down was also not helping the situation with my back either. My life was on overload. It had gotten to the point that I cried all the way to work and I cried all the way home. I did not want to go to either place. I knew I needed to make some changes in my life or I was going to collapse. I had even considered giving up my position as the Chief Technologist of the Cardiac Cath Lab to help reduce my stress levels. We had hired some new techs at work making it more feasible for me to come off call. There were enough techs now to cover it without my doing it. What a relief that was for me. I had also been going to school for several years working toward a bachelors degree. When Mama had first become ill, I took a leave from my educational pursuit for almost two years. Now I was able to get back into that.

Maybe I would eventually finish. I also got my time situated so that I could join the choir at church. That became my mid-week psychiatric treatment. Everyone in the choir was so nice and welcoming. And laugh . . . we always had at least one big laughing fit during rehearsal time. It became my favorite time of the week, the time I set aside for myself. It was something I was a part of that had nothing to do with my family or my work. I could go to choir practice on Wednesday nights feeling so tired and downtrodden, but when I left I would catch myself smiling all the way home.

The stress got better, but the back pain continued to be a problem. I had to take narcotics every day after I left work. I was not sleeping at night because of the constant pain. It was controlling my life so much that I felt I needed to take the drugs before I started work. I went to two orthopedic surgeons, had spinal facet injections of steroids, and wore different braces that I had gotten to improve the support of my spinal curvature when I wore my lead apron at work. The shots were wonderful, but the effects short lived. I received two shots before they told me I could not have anymore for the rest of the year because the amount of steroids used in the body had to be limited. One of the orthopedic surgeons suggested I find another job or quit working altogether. I knew those suggestions were not going to become reality in this lifetime. What was I going to have to do to get some relief? I was tired of taking narcotics all the time.

At this point, Mama took a turn for the worse. Her sugar levels were becoming more and more erratic. She started having one urinary tract infection after another. With each infection her ability to move herself became more and more difficult as she became weaker with each infection. During the Christmas season of 1998, I missed 6 weeks of work because she could not get up on her own to do for herself. I had to lift her from the bed to transfer her to her wheelchair and then transfer her back and forth to go to the bathroom. I knew how to transfer her so I would run less risk of hurting my back anymore than it already was, but she would not listen to me. Instead of holding her body close to mine when I got her up, as soon as I would get her upright her arms would start flailing around as she tried to reach for something to hold onto. It would take all the strength I had to keep her from hitting the floor. The muscles in my back were my only support and Mama's flailing was stressing them more than they were able to take. Muscle spasms would hit me sometimes in mid transfer. I even got one of my friends at work to bring my back brace that I wore at work to use when I had to transfer Mama. The brace helped me survive more back injury, but the flailing still continued no matter how adamantly I pleaded for Mama to listen to me.

Around ten o'clock one morning as I tried to transfer her in the bathroom, I snapped. When her arms started flailing, reaching for the walls or the cabinet, I immediately sat her back down and walked out of the room. I came back to stand in front of her with my hands on my hips, "Mama, if you don't listen to me and do as I ask when I try to lift you to move you to your wheelchair, one or both of us is going to end up hitting the floor. My back cannot take anymore of this abuse. Now, I want you to put your arms around my shoulders and clasp your hands behind me. I want you to keep your body as close to mine as possible and do exactly what I tell you to do, when I tell you to do it. If your hands become unclasped behind me while I try to transfer you, I will sit you back down on the toilet and you will have to stay there until Glen and Richard get off work tonight to move you."

"OK, OK," she said. I tried again.

I bent my knees and moved my shoulders toward her. She did as I told her and I moved her to the standing position. Immediately, those hands came unclasped and the flailing began. I didn't do anything but put her back down on the toilet, went into her bedroom, took off my brace and laid it on her bed. "Richard will be home at 4:30 this afternoon. If he won't move you, I'll call Glen after that. I'll bring your lunch to you at noon."

"Here in the bathroom?' she squealed.

"Yes ma'am," I calmly said.

'What am I supposed to do all this time?" I handed her a Reader's Digest and her glasses and promptly went to the kitchen to bang my head against the kitchen counter.

I started cleaning up the kitchen and washing clothes. After about a half hour, she started calling for me in this pitiful little beseeching voice like she was going to die right there sitting on the toilet. "Bel . . . . Bel . . . . come help me . . . . please."

When I went in the bathroom she asked me to try one more time to get her in her wheelchair. I in turn asked her what she was going to do when I managed to get her upright and started to rotate her to her chair.

"I'm going to hold on tight and do whatever you tell me to do."

I said, "That's all it will take, let's go." I put my brace back on and we made the transfer without a hitch. She was so excited to be back in her chair that she pulled me to her and kissed me, thanking me for doing it. Mama got over this particular instance of immobility and I went back to work a few days after this happened.

I finally went to the Cath Lab Unit Manager with the idea of giving up the Chief Technologist position and trying to work toward something that would eventually take me out of doing cases that required wearing lead and finding something I could do that would be less strain on my back. I was already taking care of the lab's inventory which I had been doing for several years. That alone was becoming at least a fifteen to twenty hour a week job. After doing

Restoring Spirit

some investigation it was decided that I would continue to oversee the inventory and could pick up twelve hours a week working with the cardiology database to try to help get the Cath Lab data entered so that we could become part of a national database for research purposes. Thus was born the position of Cath Lab Data Manager. I continued to fill in as a technologist doing cases if help was needed and the other technologists were gracious enough to relieve me so that I did not have to stay in long interventional cases. This situation was working fairly well, except when I had to stay in a case too long or perhaps work the whole schedule because staffing was short. I was managing this scenario much better than what had been going on before.

Mama's revival to mobility was short lived. She returned to her bad habits of not taking care of herself properly to control her diabetes and the urinary tract infections started up again. I talked with Glen and we both felt it was time for Mama to have more structured care than being alone during the day at my house, where she could easily cheat on her dietary needs and insulin shots. Glen and I decided to have a talk with her together.

I started. "Mama, I cannot continue to allow the abuse to my back any longer. I know you need assistance right now, but it is getting to the point that I am not physically able to continue this way. This is going to be an ongoing issue because you are going to continue to get infections because of having diabetes and are not willing to do the things you need to do to improve your health and abilities. Also, I cannot give up my job to give you the constant care and supervision you need to keep your diabetes in check. I will care for you as best I can as long as you are living here, but you need to realize that those days are becoming numbered."

Mama was quiet for a few seconds and then said to me, "Bel, I can't help it if I'm sick."

"I know that, Mama . . . but you need to understand that I can't help it if I am unable to physically give you the care you need anymore."

Glen took over at this point and gave her some of the options she had to consider. She could go to an assisted living facility right here in Bedford where she had spent a few weeks once trying to get back on her feet after an infection. She immediately refused that idea. "Those people over there aren't ever around. They don't do a thing for you but clean your room, cook your food, and give you your medicine."

"That's why it is called assisted living, Mama," Glen said. You are able to do a lot of things for yourself still. You don't need somebody to wait on you hand and foot."

"I can't see paying out all that money to somewhere that's not going to take care of you."

"OK," Glen said. We can look for another facility near here to your liking and Belvia will still be close enough to check on you often. There is another facility right here in town that Loren could walk to from school to visit you everyday.

"No, I would rather go back to Lynchburg to the Medical Care Center where I was after I was in the hospital. I know those people over there already and they look after me right." Glen looked at me and I nodded my agreement. This would locate her near the hospital where I worked and Glen lived on the other side of town. It could work.

"OK, we'll see what we can do to get you taken care of there." That encounter actually turned out to be less painful than Glen or I thought it would be. Within two weeks Glen had gotten the call from the Medical Care Center to bring her over. They had a vacancy ready for her. We got all her medical records from the local doctor transferred to the physician that would be attending her there. She told me what she wanted to take with her and I packed it. Glen and I got her moved into her room and settled in without any trouble from her at all. It was almost too good to be true. Believe me when I tell you now that if you get the feeling that something is too good to be true, it usually is.

Becoming the physical care giver for an aging parent is no picnic. No matter how good a relationship the child and parent have had over the years, that child is going to become "the bad child." I had been living as the "bad child" for three years while Mama lived in our home. I continued to be the bad child after she became a resident of the nursing home because according to her I put her there. She felt she was too far away from Loren and never got to see her enough anymore. Reminding her that had been her choice was moot. She never thought I came to see her enough even though I visited two or three times a week to spend time with her. I felt I had never really been able to please my mother and it looked as if that was not going to change now. I knew she was going to continue to badger me because she thought she could wear me down enough to take her back home with me. I was resolved in my decision not to let this bother me and basically just ignored her negativity and laughed it off as her efforts to lay a guilt trip on me continued. I would go see her regularly and took Loren whenever I could. I tried to make sure she was being properly cared for. I remained the bad child for the majority of the next 7 years and made sure I never missed a dose of my anti-depressant.

Empty Nest

After cracking your head on the bottom and banging it on a rock a few more times for good measure, coming up for air is a relief. The stream shows signs of stability and tranquility as it gently rolls into a fresh pool of gentle movement. The sun is shining again, finally. Yet, as always, the weather is ever changing.

It's often odd how you end up at a certain point in your life and start doing something you never thought you would do. When Richard and I had first gotten married in 1981, he signed us up at his church to help with the youth group without talking to me about it first. That action of itself angered me. I was even more angered because I was still in my "I don't want anything to do with God" mode. I could handle going to church on Sunday morning sometimes, but I did not want to be bogged down trying to teach kids something that I really wanted no part of.

Much had changed in me since I started attending church in Bedford during the late 1990's. I had joined the choir, which I had always refused to do in Salem. I kept the nursery regularly when the church started having an early service. I attended Sunday school, which I had not done since I was eighteen. I also opened my home to all Loren's friends so that they always felt safe there and knew they had a refuge if they needed one. I tried to assist them in their trials of youth by relating to them through experiences of my own. I tried never to say, "You shouldn't do that," but give them an experience of mine that had turned bad because I made a stupid decision. This gave them something to think about to make their own choice. I became their friend. They always allowed me to share some of their time together. Some felt they could talk to me about things they were afraid to broach with other adults. I felt honored to be able to mentor them in this way.

Bill, the associate pastor at Bedford Presbyterian, asked me if he could use our home occasionally for youth gatherings. During the summer, he often got the group together for movie reviews and dinner. I was happy to do this. Half those kids were in our home a lot anyway. There were a lot of talented young people in this youth group and others in the area at the time. One summer Bill got the idea of doing a coffee house format open mike session with area youth groups and the friends of all these teenagers. It was open to anyone who wanted to participate whether through music, dance, writing, drama, or whatever talent the youth wanted to share as long as it was appropriate. Bill invited other churches in our area and also in our local Presbytery to attend and participate as they wished. A local coffee shop just down the street from the church allowed Bill to have the event there and they would sell coffee, drinks and snacks. Richard and I volunteered to help by collecting the small cover charge at the door to cover expenses and perhaps donate the rest to a worthy cause. We had several adults volunteer to be chaperones. This venture turned out to be a big success. There were plenty talented acts signed up to provide a full evening of entertainment and more youth showed up than the coffee shop could hold. After this, Bill arranged several other "Coffee House" events that we helped with. I really didn't realize it at the time, but God was grooming me through Bill to become more active with the youth programs at church, especially the Senior High group.

In the summer of 2001, Bill called me one evening and started telling me about a new format he had in mind for the youth programs. Rather than have one or two people be responsible for everything the youth were involved in doing, he wanted to split the various portions of the ministry up and have 2 people responsible for that part for both the middle school age and the high school age youth. There were divisions made for fellowship events, camps and conferences, worship and ministry, Youth Sunday, and the Christmas service. Bill asked me if I could commit to any of these. I was reluctant to commit mainly because my job usually took more hours than actually specified. My mother, while no longer living with us, still demanded a lot of my time and attention. I was also still working on classes to receive a baccalaureate degree someday. All were good excuses, I thought. I told Bill I really didn't feel I had the time to make such a major commitment. I would help out as I could with the use of my home or being a chaperone as needed for the Senior High youth, but just could not commit to the rest. Bill was very gracious about my refusal and I didn't think I would hear anymore about it.

After that at various functions I would attend, Bill would use any opportunity to intentionally state within my hearing range that it was a shame that some people just did not have time to devote to the needs of the youth. I would chuckle and smile at him to let him know I heard his little dig at my refusal. Over several weeks, the thought kept popping in my head that maybe I could arrange to be off from work the week the Senior Highs went to Montreat, North Carolina to the youth conference and could attend as a youth advisor for that. I felt I needed to ask Loren if that would be alright with her or if she would rather I not be there since it would be her last trip to Montreat as a member of the youth group.

When I asked Loren about it, she was delighted that I was thinking about going to Montreat with her. She loved that place so much that she was ecstatic that she would be able to share it with me. Her friends in the youth group seemed positive about my going as well. On the next Sunday morning after I had received the blessing of the youth group, I caught Bill after church and told him I would go to Montreat as a youth advisor, but that was all that I could commit to. He reminded me that there were fundraisers involved with that and I agreed to help with that as well. Erin's mother, Karen would be the other adult in with the camps and conferences and we could work all the details out. He looked me straight in the eye, balled up his right fist and pulled it in tight to his right side with a whispered but very audible, "Yes!" Bill had successfully snagged me with his hook and reeled me in.

At the end of the summer, Bill had a meeting with all the adults who had volunteered to help with his new youth program format. Each division had specific responsibilities for various projects during the year. Each division had adult and youth members to work together to facilitate each part. Bill had made packets with previously used flyers and any other information on each division that he had on a floppy disc for us to refer to. This arrangement got eight to ten adults involved with the middle and high school kids instead of just four. In the fall when school started, there was a kick off event for the youth getting back into the routine of regular activities as a group after summer vacation. These divisions were presented to them as well as the people who would be spearheading the divisions. All went well and we all felt good that this arrangement would work for everybody and not dump everything for the entire year on four volunteers and Bill. Karen and I talked about what we could do for some different fund raisers for camp registrations and sat back and watched for a while since our division would not really need to kick in until we started getting ready for the annual Valentine's Day Luncheon the Senior High's put on to raise funds to go to Montreat.

Everything was going along smoothly. Bill got another Coffee House event together with the help of the fellowship group. The Senior Highs went to Roanoke to a game facility that had a haunted house set up for Halloween and also had various types of activities for them to participate in like rock wall climbing, go carts, pinball and such. After that event, I helped Bill chaperone a lock-in with the teenagers at the church where we all spent the rest of the night playing games and watching movies. In early November, Bill and Aimee decided to host a dinner for the Senior Highs and their parents. We were all to come bringing a dish to share for an evening of fellowship.

The dinner was scheduled for Sunday evening. Bill asked me as I was leaving church if I was coming to dinner with Loren. I told him I doubted it because I had a paper to write for a class I was enrolled in and didn't know if I could make the deadline to turn it in.

Bill said, "Belvia, we are really looking forward to having all the parents of the youth there with them."

I said, "Don't worry Bill, Richard is planning to come. I've already made a cheese ball for them to bring."

"OK, but I hope you will be able to finish your paper and reconsider joining us."

"I will if I can, Bill."

As it turned out, I did get my paper finished and ready to mail to my professor that afternoon. I told Loren that I would be able to go to dinner at Bill and Aimee's after all with her and Dad. The other parents would be there and it would be a lot of fun. When we arrived, Bill met us at the door.

"Hey, everybody. Belvia, I'm glad you could make it. It wouldn't be the same without you."

"Thanks, Bill, I just happened to get everything done." As I walked into their living room I met Aimee. We hugged and greeted each other as we always did.

"Where are Elli and Taylor?" I asked of their children.

"Oh, they're spending the day with Bob and Jo. We'll go get them later. This would probably be too much excitement for them anyway. We would never get them to bed after this," Aimee replied in her usual perky voice. I then took the cheese ball I had made and set it up in the kitchen with crackers on a tray for everybody to start eating. We all were talking, laughing and enjoying being with each other. Our children were all growing up so fast and we talked about how lucky we were to have Bill and Aimee to nurture them. This youth group was making a huge difference in a lot of young lives and giving them a great foundation to take with them when they went out into the world.

After dinner was over, Bill and Aimee got everybody to come together in their living room for a little activity. We all started gathering noisily, still talking and laughing. As we all found a place to sit, there were people covering almost every inch of the room, sitting on the furniture, perched on an armrest, leaning against the back of the couch, or piled together in the floor.

Bill and Aimee sat on the floor to one side of the room where everyone could see them. Bill got everybody's attention finally and started talking. I cannot remember verbatim what he said but the jest of what he was saying was that Aimee had been called to a church in Ashville, North Carolina and could finally become ordained as a Minister of the Word and Sacrament. Since they had both completed seminary, they had planned periodically to reassess their situation about every five years to be sure they were both getting their chance to serve God in ministry. Bill had received the first call to come to Bedford as our associate pastor. Now it was Aimee's time to be called. They were leaving us. They would be gone before Christmas.

The room was silent for a long time as we all tried to let what Bill had just said sink in. Somebody spoke up and said that even though we don't want them to leave us we need to remember to be happy for Aimee. The three girls who would be graduating from high school the next summer, Katie, Erin and Loren were devastated. The three of them left the room in tears. We all were in tears. All I could think of was that this great youth group was going to fall apart because they were going to lose their little red haired, guitar picking pied piper. They were all so attached to Bill and Aimee. This was going to be so hard for some of these kids to deal with. So many times I had heard Loren say when thinking about doing something that perhaps she shouldn't, "Oh, I better not do that. Bill wouldn't like it." How were we all going to get through this?

I finally attempted to speak up and tell Bill and Aimee how much we all loved them and were happy that Aimee would become ordained as she had been wanting for so long. I tried to let them know how much they meant to all of us. I didn't do a very good job. My tears overtook me and all I could do was hug them and sob. They knew how I felt. I went to check on Loren to see how she was doing. She was sitting in the bathroom, crying her eyes out. She saw me and ran into my arms.

"Why do they have to leave, Mommy? Why?" All I could do was hold her. I had no words of wisdom now to comfort her. I, who always had an answer for everything, right or not, could not come up with anything to calm her anguish. I knew in my heart that Bill and Aimee were leaving because they felt God was asking them to move. There was somewhere else that needed their gifts more than we did. That still was little comfort.

It finally all made sense now. The division of labor, the increase in adults, the packets with all the data had been compiled and facilitated by Bill to hopefully keep everything going with the programs he had started with these youth. After Bill and Aimee's departure, Karen and I made it our mission to keep the Senior Highs together and get them to Montreat for camp. Between the two of us we got several fundraisers put together and had a successful Valentine's Day Luncheon. Karen had been told that the middle school group wasn't interested in attending the Massanetta Middle School Conference. The fellowship division seemed to be focusing on the middle school age group more, so we honed in on the senior high age group.

Thus, Karen and I inadvertently became the two advisors for the Senior High Youth group. This wasn't exactly as Bill had planned it, but Karen and I were determined to keep this group together until a new associate pastor was called to reorganize it.

It was very difficult for the youth group at Bedford Presbyterian during that winter of 2001 and spring of 2002. Bill, Aimee, and their children, Elli and Taylor moved away around Christmas 2001. The teenagers were trying very hard to keep the group together as they knew Bill would want them to. In the five years Bill and Aimee spent as part of our church family, they formed tremendous bonds with our youth and their families, started great programs and activities to keep them busy, and loved them unconditionally. We were all very happy for them and Aimee's opportunity to become ordained, yet felt a big void in the group without their presence. That sly Bill had delegated all the work out to various people so it would not fall all to one or two to insure the programs he had started would continue in his absence.

I still smile just thinking about his mission to secure the groups continuance. I also remember Loren and I cried for weeks every time we thought about their leaving us.

While my faith in God was returning, I still often had many questions when I could not figure out what He must be thinking He was doing. I knew Bill and Aimee felt called by God to make this move, but why couldn't God have waited until these three girls that were so close to them went away to college. Wouldn't that have made more sense, not to rip their hearts out right now when they are getting ready to have major life changes start happening in their lives. I suppose God thought the girls were ready to fly, but I wasn't so sure I was.

My plans to keep busy after Loren left for college were simple. I was going to busy myself in work, choir, and youth group activities. My plan had originally included Bill being the youth group leader. It had not been in my plans to be a leader, only an advisor. I pondered how I might be able to accomplish this task. I finally decided not to worry about it. I had treated those kids like they were my own all the time I had known them. I would just continue to do that. My parenting skills seemed to have worked alright with Loren. Maybe it would work for the youth group, as well.

On a chilly Saturday afternoon in February, 2002, the phone rang. "Hey Belvia, this is Russel. Is the old man around?"

"Sure, Russell, he's out in his house; let me get him for you." The old man, my husband Richard, was in his hideaway above his garage/workshop. I knew exactly what he'd be doing when I went out there to tell him the phone was for him. The television would be on, tuned to the *New Yankee Workshop* as his hero, Norm, explained the finer points of woodworking. Richard would be riveted in his recliner, snoring like he was taking solid oak trees down with a chain saw. Evidently, this method of gathering knowledge works well for Richard because he can build anything.

I climbed the stairs to find him exactly as I had expected. "Honey, the phone is for you. It's Russell."

He woke groggily, "Huh, Russell who?"

"Carrie's dad, from church," I explained.

"Oh, OK." As he started to get up, I made my way back to the house.

A few minutes later, Richard came in to get his coat and car keys. "I'm going to the church. Russell wants me to go up in the steeple with him to look at the bell cradle. He thinks there's something wrong with it."

The sanctuary of Bedford Presbyterian Church was built in the pre-Civil War era. The façade of this structure and its steeple have been a landmark in the center of this small, quaint little town since 1844. The original structure had two large doors that opened directly into the sanctuary, which are still there today. To the sides of the front entrance there were doors opening to stairs that led to the balcony from the outside of the church. Originally, the balcony was not accessible from the inside of the church. Before the Civil war, the slaves would enter these outer doors to the balcony. They were not allowed to enter the main sanctuary of the church. Eventually, these doors were closed up and stairs were built from the inside of the sanctuary to reach the balcony. Other than this, a few coats of paint and the addition of an organ, the main structure of the sanctuary is as it was in 1844.

About an hour and a half later, Richard walked back into the house, shaking his head. "What did you find out?" I asked.

"If they don't stop ringing that bell, it's going to fall down through the ceiling above the front door of the church and kill somebody."

The Worship Committee, of which I was a member at the time, met on the following Tuesday. The metal hardware that allowed for the ringing of the bell and the wood that housed it were worn out from years of use and moisture. We were being advised that the bell should not be rung again until the cradle was fixed. We voted to stop the ringing of the bell until further notice and as good Presbyterians always do, we formed a sub-committee to research restoring the bell cradle to its original status.

The bell that had been rung to call the town of Bedford to worship God at 10:45 every Sunday morning since 1844 was silenced. With any knowledge of Presbyterians at all, anyone would expect it may be a long while before the bell would ring again.

Karen and I had been busy helping the Senior High Youth group try to raise funds to go to Montreat, a picturesque retreat in North Carolina, where our much expanded youth group loved to attend camp during the summer. Karen's husband, Joseph, our Senior Pastor, would help us as he could, but was extremely busy with Bill gone. We had thirteen youth signed up to go with us in July. Everyone had been working really hard on our fundraising projects and Karen and I wanted to get the group together just to have a little fun. Her son, Caleb, a member of the youth group, had his 16th birthday coming up. Karen decided to have a cookout for the group going to Montreat and also make it a surprise birthday party for Caleb. With everyone's school, sports, or work commitments, Sunday afternoon seemed the best time for the event.

The appointed Sunday, April 28, 2002 was a nice spring day, warm and sunny, the perfect day for a cookout. The colors and scents of spring had been becoming increasingly evident in the past few weeks. The fragrance of lilacs was wafting through the air as the bright green of newly fertilized grass was a vivid backdrop for the tulips, daffodils, dogwood and redbud blossoms. After church, I went to the grocery store to pick up a few items to prepare food to take to the cookout. Later while I was in the kitchen cooking, I noticed the sky darkening for the onset of a springtime thunder storm. These little storms were not uncommon for this time of year and I knew it would probably be over before the cookout was to start. Suddenly, a very strong wind started to blow out of the west. The trees were bending over from the force of the wind and the rain started coming down in sheets, the wind making it look that much more wicked. It started hailing and the electricity went out. It was a good thing I had just finished cooking. I remember thinking I would be glad when this little storm was over. It was wreaking havoc on my young spring plants coming up in the garden. That hail would rip big holes in my hosta leaves. I wouldn't get to enjoy them anytime at all before the deer ate them.

The storm only lasted about fifteen minutes, the power came back on, and the sun was back out making the wet grass sparkle like diamonds. Some of the lawn furniture had been blown across the deck; the bench that usually sits beside the garage door was parked upside down in the flower bed across the driveway, its legs rising upward exclaiming the grandeur of the crepe myrtle sprouting. There were some sticks and old leaves scattered across the yard, nothing unusual for a quick moving spring thunderstorm. Richard, Loren and I packed up the car with our goodies and headed toward Joseph and Karen's house. There were certainly a lot more tree limbs down in the outskirts of Bedford as we traveled to their home only a few miles away. The thunderstorm that had come and gone so quickly certainly had cleaned a lot of dead limbs out of the trees. Everybody on Oakwood Street would be doing a lot of raking tomorrow.

Joseph met us as soon as we got to the door or their home. "Richard, I'm sure glad you're here," Joseph exclaimed. "A tornado has hit downtown Bedford and one of the session members called to tell me the steeple is down in the church yard and parking lot. Thanks be to God, no one has been hurt. Will you go with me to check it out?"

The two men left to assess the damages to the church as neighbors, friends, and the teenagers of our youth group arrived to help Caleb celebrate his birthday. Life continued on as it always does, even as the church's symbol of the ascension of Jesus Christ lay on its side in the church yard.

Joseph and Richard were back for dinner. As we sat around the dining room table eating hotdogs drowned in Karen's awesome homemade chili, we talked about how the church had been working to try to come up with the funds to fix the bell cradle. I jumped into the conversation saying, "Maybe God is telling us to get to it by making the entire steeple crash to the ground."

Joseph laughed and said, "You think?"

I wondered aloud, "How are we ever going to raise the kind of funds it is going to take to restore the bell cradle and the steeple?

Joseph reassured us saying, "God will provide." And He did.

A family in our church donated the money for the restoration of the bell cradle in memory of their father who had been a devout member of our church. The church building was insured and we were told that the insurance would cover the cost of restoring the steeple to its historically correct specifications. With the hiring of a building contractor specializing in the art of historical restoration, the bell would once again ring out the call to worship in a steeple that would be an accurate reproduction of the 1844 original. God was doing his job just like Joseph said He would.

The broken steeple was cleaned up from the church yard and the bell was hauled away by the contractor who would rebuild the bell cradle. It was estimated to be about a six month undertaking for the contractors to restore the steeple. The Bedford Presbyterian Church family had been rocked by the departure of the Bill, Aimee and the children. Now within a few months the steeple had been blown to the ground. I was beginning to wonder what was in store for us next. There was no time to fret about it for very long. There was much to be done within the next few months.

May, June and July were busy months for our family. May ushered in the receipt of my BS degree that I had been working on for ten of the last twelve years. Loren always would ask me when she was little, "Mom, when are you going to graduate? I would tell her I would try to finish by the time she finished high school and that is what happened. We were both graduates of 2002. Richard, Loren and I were all into various activities and projects. Richard had started building a potting shed in the back yard and spent most evenings after work at his favorite hobby, sawing wood and hammering nails. His hobby would lead to a place I could pursue my favorite hobby, gardening. I was still actively helping the Senior High youth group at Bedford Presbyterian Church get ready for our pilgrimage to the Montreat Youth Conference in July. Loren and I also were preparing to attend the Worship and Music Conference at the same location in June. Work for me was demanding a lot of overtime to finish two major projects I was responsible for. I could do it in phases and my goal was to get to a stopping point before I went to the youth conference so that I would be ready after that to cut back on the overtime for a while and spend some much needed time with my family. Loren was graduating from high school in June and heading for the traditional "Beach Week" at Myrtle Beach, SC. We were excited about all the things going on around us and looking forward to eventually spending time together as a family to prepare for Loren to go to college. We would have the end of July and early August to shop for all Loren's college supplies for her dorm room. My work projects could then be finished after Loren was settled in college. We also found out that Richard's cousin and his wife from Texas, not only family but treasured friends of ours would be passing through Virginia on their way to New England on vacation and we would get to see them. Their arrival would not be until Loren and I had returned from Montreat in July. Great timing! I had everything planned out and under control.

Loren's graduation day, bright, sunny and beautiful, came and went with the usual pomp and circumstance. We had friends and neighbors come to our home that evening to join in our celebration of Loren's right of passage into adulthood. She and her friends left the next morning for "Beach Week." During that second week of June, I buried myself in my work projects, working overtime everyday to accomplish my goal. I always tended to dive head first into my work during life changing times to help me stay busy. That way I wouldn't think about the changes occurring as often and get upset about them. I was diligently working toward not being a weeping mother, losing her only child to college life. I needed to work toward having my own life again now that the nest would be empty. Until I could figure out what I wanted to do, work would fill the void.

Loren and her friends returned from Myrtle Beach with only one brush with the law. Richard received a call about 2am one morning from the Myrtle Beach Police Department asking for permission to release the 1991 Ford Explorer that belonged to us back into Loren's possession. It had been parked illegally and impounded. We were grateful that a parking violation and getting her car towed was the only major trauma she had to deal with and hoped it would be a lesson learned. Richard continued sawing wood and hammering nails. The potting shed was taking shape. The framing was up and it was going to have a covered front porch. I have always loved a front porch, a product of my country girl background. Perhaps a rocking chair would be good for it. Hopefully someday I would have time to sit and rock and enjoy the beauty of the flowers, birds and butterflies that God allows to inhabit my garden. Loren and I had one week after her return from the beach to get ready to attend the Worship and Music Conference. There were friends to see, work to complete, grandmothers to visit, clothes to wash and packing to do. Soon I would get a break and have an entire week to spend at Montreat with Loren. It was her favorite place on the planet and she could not wait to show it to me. She was also excited that we were going to see the Bill and Aimee while we were there. At Montreat, we would be very near where they were now living in Ashville. I shared in her enthusiasm, looking forward to this trip.

Jane the minister of music, her husband Mike, Joseph our pastor, Loren and I set out for Montreat after church on Sunday, June 23. The entire group had been preparing me for what to expect at Montreat. I knew it had to be a special place. Loren had always spoken of it as a place where life changing experiences happen. Even with their efforts to prepare me for this experience, I was still not ready for what awaited me there.

Have you ever been to a place where you feel God's presence? I had felt it when I was young in the church sitting next to Daddy. My mother and father had a lot of trials to deal with in their respective families during their marriage and also in their own family with the deaths of three of their children. When Daddy would be asked to pray during our worship service, I would feel God in his voice. With everything he and my mother had been through, he still gave praise to the Heavenly Father and asked for continued strength to surmount life's trials. Every time Daddy and Mama would go to the altar to pray and cry, I would feel God enter our little church at those times to heal their strife. It was like you could feel Him place His hands on them to let them know that He was still with them to comfort and guide them. The same feeling came to me at Montreat. I knew God was there, in all the people around me, and in that place. I could imagine God stretching out under a tree with feet crossed and hands under his head for a pillow, looking at the majesty of the surrounding mountains and at the sky that is so close you can almost touch it. He listens to the rippling water running over stones warn smooth from years residing in the creek bed. He smiles and sighs at a job well done. I imagine this place as where God takes His vacations. It could be His summer home. He may lounge around with His feet up for a time, but His servants are very busy there.

There were plenty of classes and workshops to keep us busy. Loren spent most of her time with Bill and Aimee in the class they were instructing for the youth attending the conference. Jane and I joined the choir that would be performing at the ending worship service of the week. Joseph, Mike, Jane, and I attended various lectures during the week. The ones that completely blew me away were conducted by Walter Bruggemann, a professor at Columbia Seminary. Here is this short, small, sixty-something man, balding, grey hair, mustache and beard, seeming calm enough at a glance. Yet, when he projects his voice, here is this brash roar like the growl of an old irritated lion. I thought his voice revealed what Moses would have sounded like screaming at the Israelites when he threw the tablets of the commandments down from the mountain side to destroy the golden calf. He definitely got my attention and kept it. By the end of the week, I was happy to know that some of my thoughts on the texts of the Old Testament were not as radical as I thought or perhaps Bruggeman's thoughts were just as radical as mine. Anyway, I no longer felt alone in some of my interpretations of these scriptures and found I was in good company since Joseph was as enthusiastic about the lectures as I was.

Jane and I enjoyed the choir experience as well. There is nothing like the sound made by a big choir breathing in fresh mountain air and exhaling praise to God. We got to sing from a music collection that varied in style from a soft, serious classical format to a raise the roof black gospel number. I was ecstatic to be a part of it. Singing always lifts my spirits.

The conference was over before we knew it and on Saturday morning we were Bedford bound. I was returning home feeling more spiritually aware than I had felt in years. I wasn't sure what I was supposed to do with that feeling, but I was sure it would come to me at some point. I didn't have time to think about that now. Right now, I had to concentrate on getting ready to go back to Montreat again with the Senior Highs. Loren and I had one week to get ready to return.

For Loren, it was easy. She stopped in the laundry room when she got home and emptied her suitcase of dirty clothes in the washer. After drying them, she folded them up and put them back in the suitcase. She was ready again for Montreat. Her suitcase never left the laundry room until we put it back in the car a week later.

It usually took me a day or two at work to catch up. Even though I had put projects on a back burner for a few weeks, things were progressing as planned. I was still working late every night, but knew that if I kept on plugging along I would eventually see light at the end of the tunnel. Amidst working late, pulling weeds, and cooking dinner, I managed to get my clothes washed and repacked. Loren and I stood on the back sidewalk at home one afternoon and laughed about Richard, who was on the roof of the potting shed putting on shingles. He couldn't find a bandana to wrap around his forehead to keep the sweat out of his eyes, so he had tied an entire T-shirt around his head.

The shirt looked like an oversized white turban with his bald dome protruding from the top. Loren ran for the camera to capture this Kodak moment.

In all this business, the family made it to the picnic in our church parking lot to celebrate July 4th and watched the fireworks that were set off from the D-Day Memorial. We were making nametags for everyone to wear and I fixed one for Joseph that read, "Bruggermann Wanna Be." Joseph and I enjoyed a good laugh over it. We talked about how long it was going to take to get the steeple back on the church and what a great time we had at the Worship and Music Conference. Loren and I were getting excited about our return to Montreat and Richard was looking forward to another week of peace and quiet.

I was enjoying spending so much time with Loren and the youth group at church. Watching them grow up and mature into adulthood had been a treat I never imagined I'd have. This youth group had been a pivotal influence in Loren's life, just as it had been for some of the others involved. Bill, with help from Aimee, had done a great job in guiding their evolvement to this time in their lives. The youth would be better people for it and so would I for having been able to watch it happen. My own faith was growing watching my daughter's take shape. With Bill and Aimee departing, I felt a responsibility to try to help keep the group alive until a new youth pastor could be found to lead them.

That commitment was also somewhat selfish on my part. I knew that when Loren went away to school at the end of this summer, I was going to miss her terribly. Even though she would only be forty minutes away, she would still not be in my life everyday as she had been for the past eighteen years. I hoped that becoming more active with these youth would fill that void. I made the commitment to help myself as much as I did it to help them.

On July 7, 2002, after being commissioned at the early service, Bedford Presbyterian sent fifteen of us on our way to Montreat. Five of the girls with us had just graduated from high school. This would be their last visit to the conference as members of a youth group. Everyone was excited about this trip together. The plan was for Bill, Aimee and the kids to meet us at My Father's Pizza for dinner on Wednesday.

After a week of small group meetings, energizers, recreation activities, and worship it was finally time to come home again. Just as it had for Loren, Montreat had become my favorite place on the planet. I felt renewed when we left to make the journey home. Montreat would be a place that I would return to many times in the future, but not anytime soon. I had a week to catch up on my work at the hospital and then Loren and I had a month to get her ready for college. We needed to shop for clothes, sheets, pillows, comforters, toiletries, school supplies, everything.

Work took up most of my time that next week. I had a lot of catching up to do and didn't have time that week to do any shopping. As always, I had a plan. I would stay over that week until I caught up everything and the next week I could just work regular hours and get the shopping done with Loren. After she got to school, I would be able to dive back into more work.

Bud and Susan would be here from Texas at the end of this busy week to visit Richard's family. Plans were for us to go to Salem and have dinner with them on Saturday night. On Thursday, my day off, I ran errands and bought groceries. Friday, I worked late to finish up my projects. I would clean house Saturday before we went to Salem. This dinner would be a celebration kick off to slow down for a month and get Loren prepared to move into her dorm room at the end of August.

My meticulous plans were falling into place. I had my life all figured out and it was working beautifully. I hoped by staying as busy as possible. I wouldn't have time to feel the pain that was creeping into my heart. My girl had grown up and was leaving home. She was excited and ready; I was not. I was looking forward to spending the next month being with Loren. I knew the days of lying on the bed together talking about boys and the dramas of the female teenage life were numbered. I would miss that closeness. The next month I would focus on time spent with her.

Restoring Spirit

I went to Niagara Falls once with my family. It was so beautiful to see the massive volume of water plummeting to the riverbed far below. Many were the stories of dare devils going over the falls in barrels to tempt fate, in hopes of bragging that they survived. Looking at the falls from the safety of the overlook above it on the Canadian side of the Niagara River was breathtaking in its wild beauty. The loud falling water was powerful, unstoppable. Yet, I did not fear it. We went upriver and looked down at the expanse of water leading to the abrupt drop. Rocks jutting up sporatically in the wide fast moving stream made the river look too shallow to be dumping that much water over the cliffs that I had seen from the overlook at the falls. It did not look menacing, but more like a magical entrance of shallow water into a blanket of fine mist rising up like a beautiful enchantment.

Is that how a dare devil felt when he was nearing the falls and his death? Was he entering a magical mist, feeling he was invincible? But he couldn't see the mist. He was closed up tight in a barrel not knowing when he would drop to his death. The only thing he sensed was the sound of the falls becoming louder and louder as he floated along in the swift waters. Suddenly he felt nothingness beneath him when the barrel was thrown over the edge; the only sound to be heard was the deafening roar of falling water.

"Beloved, do not be surprised at the fiery ordeal which comes upon you to prove you, as though something strange were happening to you. But rejoice in so far as you share Christ's sufferings, that you may also rejoice and be glad when his glory is revealed"
(1 Peter 4:12-13, <u>The Oxford Annotated Bible</u>, p. 1476).
"And John bore witness, "I saw the Spirit descend as a dove from heaven, and it remained on him. I myself did not know him; but he who sent me to baptize with water said to me, 'He on whom you see the Spirit descend and remain, this is he who baptizes with the Holy Spirit.' And I have seen and have borne witness that this is the Son of God." (John 1: 32-34, <u>The Oxford Annotated Study Bible</u>, p. 1285)

On Saturday July 20, I got up early and started cleaning house. I usually got frustrated and angry when I cleaned house because my family always managed to disappear or find something else they just had to do so they wouldn't have to help me. Today was no different from any other house cleaning day. Loren's room always looked like a bomb exploded in it. I shut the door. Why can't these people spit in the sink when they brush their teeth instead of all over the faucet. This is disgusting. At least at the end of this day I would get to see Bud and Susan in from Texas.

I always enjoyed these times we got to spend with Richard's cousin, Bud and his wife, Susan. We had all become close friends over the years and had great times filled with laughter when we were together. After cleaning house all day I had been refreshed by a long shower. Then I put on my make up and got dressed. I debated over what jewelry to wear. Susan and I both liked jewelry so I wanted to wear something she hadn't seen before. Loren and her boyfriend, Andrew, were going to take his car and meet us there. After finally deciding on my blings and baubles, I was ready to have fun after such a frustrating day.

People always say they have times in their lives they will never forget. That evening of more great times filled with laughter was soon to become a memory I would never remember.

What am I doing in this airport? I do wish they would turn the channel on the televisions to something besides CNN. All they keep talking about is sending troops to Iraq. Wars are bad; turn them off. As I look around, I'm thinking that these people are very strange. I don't see anybody I know. The woman standing near me has a clipboard sticking out of her neck that is being held by another woman who looks just like her. OK, where is Michael Keaton? These people are doing weird things and look like the cast of that movie, "Beetle Juice." Hopefully soon the lady smoking a cigarette in the long holder with smoke rolling out of her slit throat will walk in here and turn this bank of televisions off. I have got to get out of here.

"Where are you going, Mrs. Tate?"

"Home, I guess."

"You can't go home, yet. Put your hands back inside the rail and stop trying to get out."

I can't get up. My hands are tied down and there is some big contraption on my hand. There's Colleen.

"Colleen, get this thing off my hand." *She is looking at me like she doesn't understand a word I'm saying to her. I'm shaking my hand as hard as I can to make her understand. She still doesn't. Oh, there is that noise again. Is Jane here with the organ from church? The organ must not be working right again. She's only getting one note out of it and she sure is playing it loud. How does she expect us to sing like this?*

I'll just sit here on this washing machine and watch the clothes tumble dry in the clothes dryer. Maybe if I just hide here for a while everything will be alright.

Suddenly I woke up in a bed in a white room. It may not really have been a white room but seemed bright to me at the time. I couldn't move very much. I wanted to get up. It felt like an elephant was sitting on my chest. Was I having a heart attack? There was a rail like the bed rail on Mama's bed at the nursing home. There was an IV pole next to the bed with a gold angel wind chime and another angel made out of gold mesh ribbon hanging on it. On the other side I couldn't see anything out of the window but sky. I had been thinking at some point that I was in an airport with strange people who looked like the characters in the movie, "Beetle Juice." This sure was a strange airport and I had no idea where I was supposed to be going. Couldn't they play anything else on that television but CNN? I couldn't understand why these weird people had put an IV in my hand. There was a stuffed buzzard on the table, which many people would not understand why someone would put a buzzard in this room. Yet I immediately understood as soon as I saw it that my co-workers put it there for luck to keep me from dying. I thought to myself, "Belvia, you must be really sick." There was a woman at my bedside rolling me toward her. I remembered taking the IV out of my hand and putting the dripping angiocath into someone's pocket. I also remembered pulling another IV out of my hand, realizing I shouldn't have done it and trying to put it back. I thought if Richard ever comes I'll get him to get me out of here. I felt I really needed to get out of that room. Then Richard was there. I asked him to take me home. He shook his head and said,

Restoring Spirit

"Nope, I can't do that." Wasn't that just like Richard? I never could get him to do anything he really needed to do.

"Bel, do you know where you are?" I remember looking around the room and telling him that it looked like I was in the hospital.

"Yeah, that's right, you are," Richard told me that we had been in a car accident. "Was it my fault?"

"No, a drunk driver ran a stoplight and hit us."

"Loren?"

"Loren is OK; she and Andrew left Mama's about a half hour before we did. Do you know how long you've been here?"

"I don't know, maybe two or three days." Richard then told me it was September.

"September?" I questioned, not believing what I heard.

"Yes, September," he said. "You have been out since July 20th." I just could not fathom that I had been unconscious for so long. At some point Richard told me I had broken ribs and my lungs had collapsed. He also said my pelvis was broken. I was still in and out of sleep a lot at that point. It was probably a couple more weeks after that before I really started waking up good. I was always restless. I do remember seeing other people I knew after that.

My pastor, Joseph, would sometimes be there whispering in my ear, "I believe this has happened to you for a reason, Belvia. God must have something really special planned for you." The environment started to become less strange. There was a bulletin board hanging on the wall that I could see. My friend Sharon got the nurse to get me something to drink when I told her I was thirsty. That was the best grape juice I have ever tasted in my life. There are flowers in the window sill. It is an airport. There goes a helicopter by the window.

"Here you go, Mrs. Tate, let me clean your neck off" said the man in scrub clothes.

"Why, is my neck dirty?"

"Oh, it's just where they took the trach tube out of your throat."

"Trach tube?"

"Yes ma'am, you were on a respirator for a good while?"

"I need to get out of here now. What else are you crazy people going to try to do to me in this airport?" I think drug induced psychosis is an adequate description for my state of mind here. It's a shame I was entirely too upset to enjoy it.

I was being rolled down a hall one day when I woke up having a major hot flash. Richard was walking with me and noticed I was pulling off my covers. "Are you hot?" he asked.

"Yeah, I'm about to burn up," I told him as I tried to pull the gown away from my neck. Richard had a magazine or something in his hand and started fanning me with it. I had been having trouble seeing and couldn't figure out why for the longest time. As we were rolling down that hall, it dawned on me what was wrong. "Richard, I have got double vision."

"Oh Lord, when did that start?

"I don't know. I guess it's been since we had the accident." Accident . . . I remembered Richard told me about having an accident.

After that, I remember complaining about having headaches and feeling nauseated. I thought it may be from my vision. A doctor came and did some testing on my eyes with some portable type equipment that looked like it measured angles. As he finished examining me, he shook his head. He told us there was not much he could do right now but if it hadn't gotten better in six months to make an appointment to come see him at his office. I had seen enough doctors shake their heads that way in my career to know that he was not happy with what he saw. I felt by that action and his instructions to wait six months that I may be living with double vision for the rest of my life. This

Restoring Spirit

physician gave no other information or reason to have any hope that improvement could be expected.

I will always remember the next two stories and always laugh when I tell them. There was a therapist that started coming to see me every day. She would always wake me up, which I found rather annoying. She would start questioning me about the day of the week, the date and ask me where I was. "I don't know what day it is but I am at Lynchburg General Hospital" I would confidently tell her. That is actually where I work and thought that was where I should be if I were in the hospital.

The therapist would always say, "No, Mrs. Tate. It is Friday, September 6," or whatever day it was. "You are at Roanoke Memorial Hospital. Now you remember that and I'll see you again tomorrow." This went on for several days and I was quickly becoming tired of this young lady waking me up every day and asking me the same questions over and over again. Anyway, I knew exactly where I was. I was at Lynchburg General Hospital and there was nothing she could do to make me think otherwise.

Growing tired of this continued irritation, I decided I would take this into my own hands and get rid of this little therapist person once and for all. Next time she came in here and woke me up, I would just tell her what she wanted to hear. It happened exactly as I had intended. One morning I noticed a woman tearing the page off a big daily calendar on the bulletin board in my room. I could look at it for the day and date if the therapist came to wake me. It actually looked fairly odd to me because of my double vision. There were two calendars overlapping each other on the board. In fact there were two boards overlapping each other. The therapist came into my room a short time later, shaking me and calling me, "Mrs. Tate, Mrs. Tate wake up. I need to ask you some more questions. Are you with me? Now stay awake so we can talk. That's good, Mrs. Tate. Do you know what day it is today?

I looked over at the bulletin boards and calendars and told her, "It's Tuesday, September 10, 2002."

"That is wonderful, Mrs. Tate. I am so proud of you. Now do you know where you are?

I was ready this time. This woman was going to be history. "I am at Roanoke Memorial Hospital." Well, this young woman went ballistic; she was so delighted that I had finally answered this question to her satisfaction. She was shaking me and jumping up and down. "This is so great, Mrs. Tate. Do you realize what you've done? You know where you are."

Of course, I am thinking, "Yeah, yeah . . . . I just told you where you think I am to make you happy. I know I am at Lynchburg General. At least, maybe now you will stop waking me up with these stupid questions." You know, I never saw that young woman again. I felt so smart to have fooled her!

I still thought I was at Lynchburg General Hospital when I was being transferred from Roanoke Memorial Hospital to Virginia Baptist Hospital for rehabilitation. Lynchburg General and Virginia Baptist Hospitals are both owned by the same parent company and are both located in the city of Lynchburg, Virginia only four miles or so from each other. Roanoke Memorial Hospital is in Roanoke, Virginia approximately 80 miles from Lynchburg. The ride in the ambulance became a rough one for me. I was very uncomfortable during the long distance trip. I could not figure out for the life of me why it was taking these two guys so long to get from Lynchburg General to Virginia Baptist. It was only four miles. How could it be taking so long? Surely they were lost.

After becoming exasperated by the trip I finally asked, "Where are we?"

One of the men said, "We just got to Montvale, Mrs. Tate." Montvale is about half-way between Lynchburg and Roanoke, not too far from where I live. I went off at that point.

"What in the world are you people doing taking me all the way to Montvale to get to Virginia Baptist? It would be closer now to take me to Bedford from here. Just take me home."

"Oh no, Mrs. Tate, we can't do that. It won't take too much longer. We'll have you at Virginia Baptist in no time." Of course, what they considered no time was actually over an hour away. By the time of our arrival at Virginia Baptist, I felt like I had been beaten with a club. Every broken rib was screaming and I had a sore area on my back that felt like it was on fire. Two of my friends from work, Tammy and Sharon, met us at Virginia Baptist when we arrived. They have told me that I was raising cane when we got to my room. I was so upset that the ambulance driver had gotten lost and taken me all the way to Montvale before he realized he was going in the wrong direction and had to come back to Lynchburg to get me to the Baptist. I do remember that I had full intention of telling those men in the ambulance what I thought of that whole trip if I ever saw them again. Of course, at the time Tammy and Sharon couldn't figure out what I was talking about. They thought I was out of my mind, but I knew exactly what I was talking about.

After I was settled in bed, my friend Jenny brought my cousin Susan from Florida in to see me. I remember thinking how great that was to have them with me. I felt like I was home. I was so tired; I didn't talk much. I had finally gotten some pain medicine and went in and out of sleep. Shortly after Jenny and Susan left, Laura, one of my young friends from church came to visit and told me she was pregnant. She and I had grown close at a Disciple Bible Study class we had attended together. I felt honored that she had come to tell me her news. Then I slept for a week.

Whether it was from all the drugs I had been given to keep me unconscious for so long or the brain damage I had suffered, I didn't start being very awake and alert until the doctors gave me Ritalin to keep me awake during the day. It wasn't until then that I fully realized the extent of my injuries and medical treatment.

Rescue squad, jaws-of-life, no blood pressure, intubation . . .

Fractured liver, internal bleeding, transfusion 5 pints of blood . . .

Broken ribs, flail chest, collapsed lungs, 3 chest tubes, respirator . . .

Third space fluid shift, swollen like Pillsbury Dough Boy, just like Mama did . . .

Broken pelvis, intubation tube erosion, emergency tracheotomy . . .

Pneumonia, bronchoscopes through the chest wall both sides . . .

Suction, suction, suction lungs and trach . . .

Blood clots, pulmonary emboli, get that blood thin, thin, thin . . .

Cervical collar rubs sore on back of head . . .

MRSA . . . Methicillen Resistant Staph Aurius . . .

Double vision and a blind spot in the eyes . . .

Right arm numb from elbow to fingers . . .

Hematoma and open wound . . . back where chest tube was . . .

Feeding tube, drug induced coma seven weeks . . .

Brain damage . . .

I wasn't at all sure how this was all going to work out. I was a bit pessimistic about a positive outcome. I didn't tell my immediate family of my fears. I knew they had fears of their own. I knew it had to have been hell for them these past two months, wondering and waiting if I would ever be back with them. They probably didn't need me falling apart right now. Hell, I felt too bad to fall apart, fight, or fret about how others were doing. I just wanted to get well and not have to worry about anything else right now.

One day after the Ritalin started working to keep me more alert, I asked a nurse one day what the date was.

"It is September 28, Mrs. Tate."

"I have missed calling my aunt on her birthday!" I said distraught.

"When was her birthday?" she asked me.

"It was the twenty-third. I've called her on her birth day every year since I left home when I was eighteen years old."

"Is it a local call from Lynchburg to where she is?"

"Yes."

"Well, here is the telephone. Why don't you give her a call now? She will probably be glad to hear from you, even if it is a few days late."

My aunt Bib's birthday call had become a ritual I performed religiously in my adulthood to honor in some small way the woman who had always been my confidant for all those things kids can't talk to their parents about. Even in adulthood, she had always been there for me to talk to and bounce ideas and feelings off of. She had always hugged me, encouraged me, and told me I could do anything I set my mind to. She was my cheerleader, anchor, and support. I picked up the phone the nurse had laid in my lap in the bed. With my double vision, it took me three times to get the number dialed.

After the second ring, I heard Bib's familiar deep "Hello?"

Weakly and tearfully I replied, "Hey Bib, it's Belvia."

"Belvia!" she said with surprise. There was silence for a few seconds. "I can't believe you have called me. I should be the one calling you."

"I wanted to call you to wish you a happy birthday. I just realized today that I missed calling you like I always do."

"Lord, Belvia, with everything that you have been through, I am shocked that you remembered my birthday." She laughed her warm comforting laugh and I could envision her sitting on the love seat in her kitchen, holding the phone to her right ear and playing with the button at the collar of her blouse as she always did. "I want to come to see you as soon as I can, but I have to wait for Linda or Donnie to bring me."

"There's no rush, Bib. I think I'm going to be here for a while. Why don't you wait a week or so until I feel better and will enjoy your visit more? I still don't feel very good and I get tired real easy."

"Well, whenever you're ready, I'll come. Are you alright?"

"I'm scared, Bib," I said, breaking into tears.

"What are you scared of, Bel?"

"I'm afraid I won't be able to get out of this bed and walk again. I'm afraid I won't be able to go back to work. I'm afraid I'll end up like Mama."

"Belvia, you listen to me. You are not like your mama. You have got too much Holt in you to be satisfied giving in to this. You're a fighter. Now, you just make up your mind that you are going to get better and you will."

"OK, Bib. I'll try my hardest."

"I know you will. Now you dry your eyes and get some rest. Call me again anytime you want to."

"Alright, I will. I love you, Bib."

"Lord knows, I love you too, Bel."

Again, my beautiful little aunt had given me the boost I needed to overcome my doubts and fears of the outcome of this healing process. I would get busy getting well.

I knew I had a long recovery time ahead. It had taken five months to get Mama home that time she had been near death because of her diabetes. Also very typical of being a health care professional, I would be the worst patient on the planet for wanting to take control of my life again. The hospital staff would have probably been a lot better off if I had been kept asleep until I was well. I had not been in this kind of situation since I was fourteen years old. I did not like having to ask others to do anything for me. I had always rather do things myself. I have always been a busy woman. It is a rare moment to see me sitting around doing nothing. I'm working, gardening, cleaning, painting, reading, singing, talking, knitting, something, anything. I always told people that is what they got for making an ex-smoker out of me. I was and still am driven to get things done on time and move on to the next thing on the agenda.

Lying in this bed in the hospital was frustrating me to no end. I wanted to get well and I wanted it right now!! I had things to do. Just as people now want instant gratification, I wanted instant healing. I couldn't stand having to lie there, not able to get up for almost two more weeks because my blood was too thin. I felt even worse when the MRSA infection hit my bladder. The double vision was driving me crazy and when I covered one eye so I could try to see better, I couldn't see some of the letters in the words that were on the bulletin board in my room. I couldn't even read because of it. I had always rather read than watch television. The television now really bothered me. If any shows I tried to watch had any type of violence in them, I couldn't stand it and would turn them off. Every night the nurses loaded the pump to push my tube feeding as I slept. It usually didn't take long after it was running that I would start having extremely hot flashes like I had when Richard had fanned me with his magazine at Roanoke Memorial. The hospital wasn't running the air conditioning anymore because it was fall. I made the nurses turn the thermostat off in my room, open the window and put a fan in my room so I could at least tolerate the heat. I needed to get back to work. The inventory would be all screwed up before I could get back to work. Tammy will rearrange everything in the storeroom and Linwood will trash my office. I also had thought about how well I might get. Who was I trying to kid? I may never get back to work. I had been through a major trauma to this already compromised chest cavity of mine. I had been down over two months already. I knew I was going to have to learn to walk all over again just like I had done after I was in that cast my entire fourteenth summer. The level of oxygen in my blood would drop every time the nurses tried to take the oxygen away. I was having respiratory treatments every day. How was I expecting to get back to work? I couldn't even get to the bathroom. Yet, whenever I saw Tom, the Cath Lab Medical Director, he asked me when I was coming back to work. I always told him Monday. I had no idea which Monday, but hopefully there would be a Monday somewhere down the road.

I would vent my frustrations to Joseph whenever he would come to visit. As he had done throughout this ordeal, he whispered in my ear, "Patience . . . patience . . . healing will come in God's good time." Well, God's good timing had never been satisfactory in my book. He always took too long. I pondered my plight for a long time, envisioning one scenario after another. How could I get my healing processes that seemed to be at a standstill moving ahead? I started questioning my treatments, making suggestions to the nurses and doctors. I fully intended to get this situation under control again . . . my control. I thought I knew how to get me where I needed to be better than anyone. The frustration continued as I found nothing I was doing was making any difference. I could not control this healing process. I had no control over my life anymore. I was slowly getting to start physical therapy. I was weak and my legs hurt when I stood on them. I would be put in the chair to sit up for a while and my back would start hurting, having muscle spasms from my muscles being dormant for so long.

I wanted someone else to check my eyes again. I was referred to another physician and re-examined. This doctor told me that I probably had fourth nerve palsy from the trauma of the accident that was causing a muscle in one of my eyes not to work well. It took nerves at least six months to heal. I could come see him at his office after I got out of the hospital for some other testing to see why I couldn't see parts of words. The brain damage I received may have affected my vision and created the blind spot that was causing parts of the words I was looking at to disappear.

Jenny's house is near Virginia Baptist and she came often and tried to cheer me up. She gave me a pedicure and painted my toenails fire engine red. She would bring ice cream and snuck her cat in one night because she knew how much I loved cats. She started reading a book from the Mitford Series to me that Jane had brought. We laughed as Jenny read about when Dooley walked into the priest's house and asked him if he had anywhere to take a dump. Jenny told me one evening, "Belvia, maybe God just thought you needed a good rest." I told her, "I would have preferred a trip to the Bahamas." With my issues of double vision and the television, there were many hours to lay there with nothing to do when there was no one visiting. I started reflecting on what this whole deal might really be about.

I thought about what Joseph had whispered in my ear as I woke from my drug induced slumber. "Belvia, I believe this has happened to you for a reason. God must have something really special planned for you." I wondered how God could have allowed this to happen to me and for what reason.

"Truly I say to you, He who puts his faith in me will do the very works which I do, and he will do greater things than these, because I am going to my father. And whatever request you make in my name, that I will do, so that the Father may have glory in the Son. If you make any request of me in my name, I will do it. If you have love for me, you will keep my laws. And I will make prayer to the Father and he will give you another Helper to be with you for ever, even the Spirit of true knowledge. That spirit the world is not able to take to its heart because it sees him not and has no knowledge of him: but you have knowledge of him, because he is ever with you and will be in you. I will not let you be without a friend: I am coming to you." (John 14: 12-18, The Oxford Annotated Bible, p. 1306).

Loren called me the afternoon of October 3, 2002 to wish me a happy anniversary. Her father and I had been married 21 years. Loren was in college now. She had to start her freshman year with her mother unconscious, on a respirator, in an intensive care unit. I had missed going shopping with her to get things for her dorm room. I had missed helping her move and decorate her room. I had missed crying the tears of a mother watching her only child leave the nest. I had not been there for her to talk to when she got homesick. I had missed meeting all the girls in her dorm. I thought to myself, "Belvia, you have missed all this time with Loren at this crucial time of her young life. Yet, you have only really missed a couple of months. You are so fortunate to even be alive, to have the chance to hopefully see her graduate from college, get married, and have children of her own. It was a miracle she was born and you were chosen to be her mother. God has given you another miracle here, another chance to be there for her." I knew at that point that it really didn't matter what recovery had in store for me. God already had a plan for all of us. I just needed to let Him follow His plan and accept what was to be. So many people had been praying for me during this time. I felt those prayers lifting me up to God as they had been since July 20. After all the agonizing and frustration, I finally did what I should have done a long time ago. I prayed.

"Gracious Heavenly Father, I thank you for allowing me to remain here on earth. I have been stubborn and ignorant to think that I could do anything in this life by myself. I regret that I have had to nearly die to make me understand what trust and faith in You are. The gift of forgiveness You have given us in your Son, Jesus Christ is a blessing beyond compare. I will place my trust in you, Lord, and put my life in your hands. Whatever Your plan for my healing is, I will be grateful for it and accept whatever you have in mind for me. I will make the best of whatever you physically leave me with. I will be your servant. Amen."

At the instant I ended my prayer, I felt like a surge of energy rushed through my body from head to toe. I knew the Holy Spirit had entered me, body and soul. I welcomed His presence with open heart and mind. From that point the frustration and fear left me and I felt such an overwhelming sense of peace. This feeling of joy, of having my burden lifted was so wonderful that I wasn't sure how I could ever describe it to anyone. Yet, I knew this feeling. It had been here before. It was present when Daddy would go to the altar at church. It came to me at Becky's church after Daddy died and I had rejected it. But accepting it was a powerful experience. It is a unique feeling that is difficult to put into words.

One of my brothers in Christ, Robert, who is a minister at Galatia Presbyterian Church in Eagle Rock, Virginia talked one day about how life was so full of things to do and accomplish that we sometimes cannot figure out how to fit everything into this life. He illustrated our life as a glass jar we would fill. To fill it we had priorities. Some of the priorities were sizeable rocks. These represented what we thought were the big things in our lives. This we felt were God, helping others, family and home. These would be represented by rocks we could put in the jar, God being the largest rock. Our work, civic responsibilities, extra activities, sports, whatever constituted our personal wants and desires would be represented by smaller gravels and dirt. If we felt we should put ourselves above everything else, we would put the small gravels and dirt in our jar first. Into the jar went the gravel and dirt, which filled it to about half full. Then if we tried to put the rocks of the most important things in our lives into the jar, they wouldn't all fit. There was not enough room for everything to fit in our lives this way. Nothing else much could get into the jar even if we wanted it to. He tried to pour water into the jar, but it bounced off the rocks on top and couldn't go in the jar. Yet the jar was still not completely full. Something was missing. There was still empty space in the jar of life, just as in our own lives. This was when Robert showed us what would happen if we got our priorities straight. He took everything out of the jar. We needed to switch our priorities. We should put the rocks representing God, helping others, family and home in the jar with the largest first. That way rocks all fit in the jar. Then we could put in all our personal stuff. Into the jar went the gravel and dirt. That all fit as well. Now look. There is room left over in your life. Robert picked up a pitcher of water and poured it into the jar of rock, gravel, and dirt. This is what it is to have your priorities straight and have the emptiness in your life filled with the love of God.

This was how I felt lying in the hospital bed that day. The rushing waters of God's love felt like a physical phenomenon as the Holy Spirit came into my presence. I felt filled up. I felt complete joy. This was what I had expected to feel when I was baptized those many years ago This was the joy that would put a smile on my face that wouldn't go away. I felt whole. Even in my broken physical state, I felt whole. I wasn't sure how my family and friends would react to this epiphany of the Holy Spirit that I was experiencing. I felt the need to keep it to myself for a while, at least until I sorted it out. Yet, there was no way I could ever hide the smile on my face. I knew God would not intend for me to keep this experience quiet forever. It would be told someday, somehow. But for the moment, I just lay there with my eyes closed savoring the experience. It was so awesome to realize that I was receiving this wondrous grace, this gift of the Holy Spirit, even in my unworthiness. That was the first time I had ever really felt that I was forgiven. God was in charge now and I was so relieved of all my burdens from the disappointments of childhood to the responsibility of feeling the need to be in control of my own destiny.

That moment was when I started to feel the healing begin. I felt I should concentrate on one problem at a time. I would pray about a chosen issue I felt led to pray about. I would concentrate all my efforts to regain one skill or heal one wound at a time. As I did this, things gradually started to happen. It seemed each day I regained a skill I thought was lost. Loren would call me everyday and I would tell her what feat I had performed that day.

"I stood up today . . . I walked to the door . . . I made it all the way to the nurses station . . . I got the bandage off my head today . . . everything was like doing it as a child for the first time. The littlest things delighted me from that point on. It is amazing how wonderful it feels to go to the bathroom and wipe your own butt. I made the nursing assistant laugh out loud when she came to help me back to bed after that glorious event. I was so grateful for every small step forward.

While I was unconscious, Loren had started making albums of all my get well cards so I could look at them later in the hospital when I felt better. Many of them she had torn in half and put in an album page so that I could look at front and inside at the same time without taking them out of the book. She put pictures of my flower garden in full bloom as they had been during the summer I slept, assuring me that all was well. There were also pictures of my kids scattered throughout the cards. Loren was my only child, but I had adopted all of her friends and the church youth group as my own. The cats and dog were there too. As I looked at one of the books one day after I had gotten home from the hospital, I found a piece of paper that Loren had written on stuck between the pages. It had been written about a week after God graced me with the power of the Holy Spirit. It read:

"Life, as ironic as it is, exploded into a seemingly unbreakable world. "I went to a wheelchair safety meeting today," she said with a chuckle. This, a woman who has worked in hospitals for over twenty years. Almost back to her true form, but not quite yet. "I walked 150 yards today and ate half my lunch," she boasts. This woman who once kept up with me never losing stamina. "Don't you love my sexy gown?" she asks, over-washed and faded as it is. Her inside voice is back and luscious, her body will too be home soon. Though her weaknesses hinder her tired, healing bones, flesh, she is stronger than one who eats their Wheaties, stronger than those children popping Flintstone vitamins. She cries for joy of her smallest triumphs because she is Wonder Woman to me."

Loren
October 9, 2002

Restoring Spirit

Of course, I think my daughter is the best writer on the planet, fragments and all. That is my job as her mother and probably why she thinks I am Wonder Woman. Loren has always used her writing as an outlet or a documentation of something she has observed. In finding this writing, I knew she had noticed the change in me. The days of my frustration and impatience were over and the days of praise for the simplest gifts given by God had begun.

It wasn't long before I was moved from skilled care to the rehabilitation unit for more extensive physical therapy. Joseph called one morning and asked if I would like to have communion. I was overjoyed to have the chance. He told me he would bring Janet, a church elder, to help serve communion and share in the experience. Janet was one of the newer members of our church who had been an elder at her previous church. I had met her but did not know her very well. I had first seen her walking with her husband near the library in town. She had her arm through his and had a big smile on her face. I noticed that she seemed to be blind. She and her husband, Bill, started coming to our church a few weeks after that. I introduced myself to her, trying to make her feel welcome and would make an effort to speak to her whenever I saw her again. I found out that she was indeed blind, but could see some from a small portion of her visual field. Joseph's bringing her to visit me was quite intentional on his part.

I was very glad to see them when they arrived in my room. I didn't get many visitors during the week days and often felt lonely. Joseph got chairs for them and we all sat in a circle between my bed and the window.

Joseph got things started, "Belvia, Janet has a story to tell you that I think you will find quite interesting. She has had some of the same experiences you're having right now. Janet, are you ready to share your story with Belvia?"

"Yes, Joseph. Belvia, when I was a freshman in college, I was in a terrible car accident. The car swerved and hit a telephone pole directly in front of where I was sitting in the front passenger seat. When I finally woke up, I could not see at all. My skin around my eyes was so damaged that when my eye lids healed they were healed shut. The doctors finally were able to slit my eyelids so that I could open them again. After that was done, I realized that I could see a little. I can see shadows and light and there is one point in my field of vision that I can read some if the print is large. I felt so happy to be graced by God to be alive and now He had blessed me with a small portion of my vision. Even though it was difficult, I eventually went back to college. I had many of my textbooks on tape that I could listen to and the professors were very wonderful to help me. Bill and I had gone to high school together. After he heard I was in an accident, he came to visit me and we've been together ever since. So you see, God has a plan for all of us and He is so good. He has guided me through the toils and troubles of my entire life and sent me everything I needed to survive. I praise Him everyday that I am alive."

I was in awe of this woman. I felt that my frustration over my vision was nothing compared to what Janet had survived and was embracing as the way God planned it. I now really felt blessed to be able to see, even if it was double. It is better to see two of everything than none at all. I knew if Janet could conquer her blindness with God by her side, I could deal with my vision problems. I could see God's peace in her heart by the smile on her face. It was the same peace I now had, the same smile I now had. Great joy filled my heart as Joseph prepared communion for us. As I partook of the bread and wine, I felt so honored that God had sent us His Son that we could be forgiven. Through Jesus' broken body and shed blood, we would gain eternal life. Tears streamed down my face. This communion shared with my pastor and friend, Joseph and this remarkable woman, Janet, was the most moving and memorable communion experience I have ever had. Now every time I go to Christ's table, I think of that day the three of us shared in the feast of the Father, the Son, and the Holy Spirit. Just as on that day, tears still come to my eyes as I think of how blessed I have been.

I now have a different feeling about the sacrament of communion than I used to. I grew up in a church that only served communion quarterly. I was taught that any more often than that would make the sacrament seem ordinary, less meaningful, too mundane. That was my notion until I accepted the entrance of the Holy Spirit into my life and decided to live by God's plan instead of my own. Now, I will gladly take communion anytime, anywhere. If Jesus was willing to die on the cross that I might have eternal life, I will gladly accept His flesh and blood in grateful thanks to remember His sacrifice.

I was as close to death as I could possibly get without actually getting Saint Peter to punch my ticket. I don't remember the accident. I don't remember seeing the other car coming toward us, although I assume I probably did by the strange nerve sensations I still have in my right arm. I have a habit when someone else is driving of reaching for the armrest on the passenger door if I see something that concerns me. I suppose if I am not driving, I intend holding on to something for a feeling of security. As I reach for the passenger door rest when I'm riding in a car now, that strange nerve impulse is triggered.

I don't remember going out to dinner with the family that night or taking a ride in Bud and Susan's new car. It took me several weeks to remember that I had returned from Montreat with the Senior High Youth only a week before the accident. It took me several months to get what had happened that summer just before the accident in chronological order. The accounts of family, friends and co-workers had to fill in what I missed. I don't remember any really severe pain, except for the ambulance ride to Lynchburg and a few headaches. I never would have known my pelvis was broken if someone hadn't told me. My ribs caused some discomfort when I breathed. I still feel twinges, and probably always will, where all those ribs were broken. They are still tender when touched. I cannot tolerate my cat walking across my chest anymore and am still very tender over the lower front ribcage as it now curves inward just below my diaphragm. But to say that I experienced excruciating pain at any time during this ordeal, I cannot. The drug induced coma I was kept in took care of all that. The only time I even considered that I was dead and might be in hell was when the people coming in and out of my room looked like the "Beetle Juice" cast of characters. I do hope that was the drugs and not really hell.

> When the world spins crazy
> When the world spins crazy,
> > spins wild and out of control
> > spins toward rage and hate and violence,
> > spins beyond our wisdom and nearly
> > > beyond our faith,
> When the world spins to chaos as it does now among us . . .
> We are glad for sobering roots that provide ballast in the storm.
> So we thank you for our rootage in communities of faith,
> > for many fathers and mothers
> > > who have believed and trusted
> > > as firm witnesses to us,
> > for their many stories of wonder, awe, and healing.
> We are glad this night in this company
> > for the rootage of the text,

> for its daring testimony,
> for its deep commands,
> for its exuberant tales.
> Because we know that as we probe deep into this text . . .
> > clear to its bottom,
> > > we will find you hiding there,
> > > we will find you showing yourself there,
> > > Speaking as you do,
> > > > governing,
> > > > healing,
> > > > judging.
> And when we meet you hiddenly,
> > we find the spin not so unnerving,
> > > from you the world again has a chance
> > > > for life and sense and wholeness.
> We pray midst the spinning, not yet unnerved,
> > but waiting and watching and listening,
> > for you are the truth that contains all our spin. Amen
> (Brueggemann, p. 76).

Recovering

The pool just below a waterfall can provide a respite, a place to float aimlessly in the sun to rejuvenate after surviving such a tremendous fall. There is time for reflection, time to come to terms with the situation at hand, time to become accustomed to a new found sense of peace. The stream will not always be smooth. Even now I see rapids ahead and bears reaching under the fast water plucking out fish like me for their dinner.

The days ahead were not all fun and games from that fabulous October day forward. This experience of being filled with the Holy Spirit was exactly what I needed to get my head and heart in the right mindset to learn patience with God's timing and to strengthen my perception of how He was actively working in my life. It was another month of skilled care and physical therapy before I was to leave the hospital for home. I think learning to eat again was one of the most difficult things I had to face. It was hard to eat when I wasn't hungry. I was still being fed 3,000 calories through a feeding tube during the night and I was expected to try to eat during the day. With the caloric intake I had with the feeding tube, my weight had not dropped very much. In the process of going from feeding tube to eating again, I lost about ten pounds before I went home and another fifteen pounds after that. Hunger was a sensation I would not experience again for two years. Now, I still only feel hunger when I haven't eaten all day and sometimes not even then.

One of the physical therapists who started working with me at first told me that he bet I would walk out of the hospital. It was a very slow process. I had been in bed for two months. At first, I thought there was no way that I would be able to walk myself out of the hospital. Yet, after realizing God was with me, I had confidence that I could do this. Other people did it all the time. Even I had done it before, only then I was fourteen and healthy, not forty-nine and feeling like I had been run over by a steam roller. Getting up was not bad, but my feet felt like the bones were coming apart and my leg muscles cramped. I had a tremendous fear of falling. I knew falling would be very painful with my ribs having been broken in so many places. I also knew that I would not be able to get up from the floor without help. I think that bothered me more than anything, being helpless and dependant on others. With a couple of weeks of exercise and some assistance from another therapist to show me I still had the ability to compensate when I felt off balance, walking came back to me. Yet, I was still weak and my stamina would be something I would have to continue to work on for a long time.

My vision was going to be an issue for at least six months. The double vision I was experiencing was from nerve damage. Nerves take at least 6 months to heal and until given that time for the healing process to be complete, it would not be known to what point my vision would correct itself. Another problem with my vision was that I had acquired a blind spot in my left peripheral vision from right occipital brain damage which either occurred at the time of the accident or when I had complications with blood clots while I had been unconscious. I really wasn't given any explanation of what could be done, if anything, to correct either of these conditions. I was very upset about my vision. I was an avid reader and was struggling with the thought of how I was going to be able to occupy my time or even go back to work with these visual problems. I would have to be patient and wait until the end of January 2003 for the nerve healing process to be complete. I hoped the Holy Spirit was up for this task of teaching me patience. Tom always said during procedures we would perform together that patience is a virtue. Unfortunately, it is not a virtue I possess.

The only way I could see single images was to close one eye or the other. I asked one of the many physicians who were attending me if patching one eye would be alright. It was suggested that I alternate patching the left eye, then the right eye so that one eye would not tend to weaken. Of course, I was not given anything to accomplish this with. One of the nurses put bandaging tape over one of my lenses on my glasses. I asked Richard to go to the drugstore and see if he could find an eye patch I could use on either eye. This he did and I became a pirate. All I needed now was the hat.

I actually already had a hat which was a turban of bandages wrapped around my head to cover the hole in my scalp at the back of my head. This had come from rubbing my head against a cervical collar placed on my neck after the accident. I learned this wound was where my MRSA infection had originated. This bandage was changed daily and the wound finally healed enough to remove the bandage about three weeks before I returned home. Another wound was not as cooperative.

At some point before I was transferred from Roanoke to Lynchburg, my chest tubes were removed. One of these tubes had been inserted just below my scapula through my right posterior rib cage. I was on blood thinning medication. After that chest tube was pulled, a hematoma formed around the wound. This was very painful and created a wound that was a hole inside of another hole. Whenever the wound needed to be cleaned, it would burn like fire was on my back. Keeping it clean was an issue because of the malformation the hematoma caused. I remember at Roanoke Memorial being turned over by nurses to show the wound to a physician. I remember hearing him emphatically say, "I'm not draining that thing again." After being moved to Lynchburg, treatment was started using a machine to flush the wound out every day to keep it clean. Slowly, the wound started healing from the inside out as was needed. It would need daily treatment for an extended period of time but had healed to the point that it could be flushed with a syringe by hand before I left the hospital. My insurance was balking on providing any nursing care after I went home. It was decided that Richard could do this at home every evening once I got discharged and the nurses showed him how to take care of it.

The physical therapist who had started my treatment would have won his bet. On Friday morning, October 18, 2002, exactly ninety days after our trip to Roanoke for dinner, I walked down a ramp at the back of Virginia Baptist Hospital to get into my mother's car, Ol' Blue, for the ride home. The nurse's aide I had made laugh out loud on skilled care saw me from an upstairs window and yelled down to me from above. "Mrs. Tate, look at you. How are you doing?"

I turned and looked up at the window, "I'm finally going home."

"Wait a second then, I'm coming down there." She came down and we stood there in the sun hugging each other and crying, not knowing if we would ever see each other again. Yet, knowing we had shared a time in our lives when a miracle had occurred. Someone who should not have lived through the injuries her body had received was walking to the car to go home.

We had kept Mama's Oldsmobile, Ol' Blue, all these years since she could no longer live alone. It was the only vehicle we had that she and I could manage getting her into and out of by ourselves. My car was too small. She could fall into it, but it would take a crane to get her out. Glen's car was too tall. Mama could fall out of it fairly well, but couldn't step up into it and had to be lifted, which we learned a long time ago she didn't submit to very well. Outings with my mother could get comical at times. And of course, she wanted to keep her car. It was her last symbol of independence. Thus, it became laughingly known as the crip's car. Little did I know I would become the crip. It was nice riding home though, even if it was in this faded blue memory of hard times gone by. It was a bright sunny day; the leaves were turning the beautiful yellows, reds, and oranges of fall. I silently thanked God as we rode toward the Blue Ridge Mountains for giving me the opportunity to see those mountain peaks again, even if there was two of everything. I could hardly wait to get home to see Gertie, our basset hound and Claire, Patches and Aggador, our cats.

As the car approached the house, I noticed something odd about our yard. There were yellow streamers hanging from all the trees and shrubs. There were balloons tied to the mailbox, the outside lights and the outdoor furniture. To add to that, there was what appeared to be about 50 pink flamingos staked on the front lawn with balloons tied to some of them as well. A sign welcoming me home from my neighbors was posted near the garage door. A card let me know that the flamingo flock was from a donation made in my honor by my co-workers. What a welcome home. In her usual welcoming manner to see who had arrived that could feed her, Claire met me at the car as I opened the car door with her big purr and her squeaky meow. I was overjoyed to touch her furry head.

As I walked into the house, my daughter and her dorm mates at school had decorated a big poster that they had all written notes on welcoming me home. Loren had class that morning but would be home later in the afternoon. It was a surprise for everyone that I was coming home this particular day. Originally, they had thought it would be the next week. Loren had rushed down before she had class to place the poster in the kitchen so it would be there when I arrived. She came home from school when her classes were over and stayed the weekend. I made her sit beside me a lot so I could hold her hand and have her tell me all about school.

My mother-in-law, Becky, also came to stay for the weekend to be sure I could take care of myself enough to be home alone while Richard worked during the week. I was glad to have her there because I was not at all sure how I was going to handle being home. She tried to wait on me, but I would have none of it. I realized I was ready to be on my own again. On Saturday night, our neighborhood was having their annual barbecue, where all the people on our street get together to eat and catch up on what was happening with everyone. I had made it home just in time to attend. It was such a joy to be with my friends again, to sit in Winnie and Earl's kitchen and listen to the laughter of life. I felt welcomed back into life with the open arms of my family, neighbors and friends. Earl said a prayer to bless the food and brought tears to my eyes as he thanked God for putting me back in their company. I knew then that in the short time we get to spend here on earth that the most important thing to cherish is relationship . . . relationship with God, family and friends. Nothing else really matters if you don't have those relationships in your life.

The next few months were spent walking around in circles, literally. The winter was harsh that year and my driving skills were sketchy at best with my visual problems. I could see to drive with my eye patch on, but vision using only one eye has no depth of field. Sometimes people would ask me if I wanted to go out to lunch with them or go to the store just to get out of the house. The weather was often too bad to get outside, so I did my own physical therapy by walking around in our house. Our foyer, living room dining room and kitchen are connected in a circle. I would walk round and round that circle more and more each day. At first, I could only manage three or four circles at a time and then had to rest. My breathing ability was much more limited than it had been before. Gradually, I was able to walk the circle in the house for an hour at a time without stopping. Stairs were a much harder undertaking. I could breathe fairly well walking on flat surfaces, but climbing stairs and walking uphill were challenges for me and still are.

I also started doing exercises with my eyes when I would go to bed at night. I would look at the ceiling and move my eyes from corner to corner, side to side, and up and down. In doing this, I noticed that in certain positions my vision was better than others. If I looked straight up and to the right, I could see single images with both eyes open. The crown molding in the bedroom would be a single image with my eyes up and become divided as I move my eyes down to the center. The same was true if I moved my eyes to look down. The double image would become one if I moved my eyes down and to the left.

Throwing my head back while I was sitting up and looking down my nose gave me single vision with depth of field that I could use for driving. I started watching television by dropping my head and looking up at the television which accomplished the same effect. I also found that I could see to paint if I held whatever I was painting up against my chest and looked down at it. Jane, the choir director, took me to the craft shop to buy wooden birdhouses and painting supplies. I embarked on a project of painting birdhouses to sell for the

Restoring Spirit

youth group at church to raise money to go back to Montreat the next summer. This was great therapy for me. It kept my mind occupied while I waited for my body to slowly heal.

I had an appointment the first week of December for a check up with Dr. Waller, the rehab physician who had facilitated my therapy in Lynchburg and had discharged me from the hospital. Our friend, Joyce, drove me to Lynchburg for the appointment. She parked in the parking garage and we had to walk up a long incline to the hospital. I had to stop a couple of times to rest before we got to the building, but I got there on my own steam. When we got to Dr. Waller's office, we were escorted to an examining room to wait. When she entered the room, I smiled at her and said, "Hey, Dr. Waller."

She exclaimed, "You look like a million bucks!"

"I feel like a million bucks," giving her by biggest grin. She put her hands to her face, excused herself and walked out the door, closing it behind her. Joyce and I looked at each other and expressed concern that something was wrong. Dr. Waller returned to the room in a couple of minutes and apologized, "I'm sorry for running out like that. I just was overcome with emotion and was going to cry. It is not very often that we get to see our patients recover as well as you have, Belvia." Joyce and I both sighed with relief that nothing was wrong and we all laughed and shared our amazement at my recovery.

Gradually, I was gaining strength. In mid-December my weight drop finally leveled at 106 pounds, twenty-four pounds lighter than I had been in July. As my strength returned, I got brave enough to put my patch on my eye and drive to Wal-Mart or the grocery store, which were not too far away from home. I then put a piece of frosted scotch tape across the mid visual field of one lens of my glasses. This way I could see single images straight ahead with only one eye. As I drove, coming upon someone in front of me, I could throw my head back and look down my nose to get my depth of field so I wouldn't rear end someone. I still had my doubts about my ability to ever go back to work. Whenever I tried to cover one eye or the other to read, gradually my vision would dim, like someone was slowly turning down the light. I'd switch the patch to my other eye. The same thing would happen. No one would explain why it was happening or seemed too concerned about it. I just could not wear the patch or read for very long periods of time. The dimming would correct itself after I would take the patch off and close my eyes for a while. Since my vision and ability to read and work on a computer were going to have to be my greatest assets in the work place, I was becoming more and more concerned about having to remain on disability, not being able to function in any capacity at work. I had spent countless hours thinking about how our family would survive without my salary. I knew I would have a disability income if necessary, but it would not be the total amount of my income when working. I worried that Loren would not be able to stay in college where she was.

Shortly before Christmas, my co-workers asked me to come to the hospital for lunch. Richard was working that day and they had invited Loren and Glen, my brother, to come. It never dawned on me that something was up. I just thought it was so nice to be together with everyone again. After lunch, Mary, our unit manager, got up and told me they had something for me.

"Belvia, the hospital has a program called Helping Hands. If a department raises funds to help a co-worker in need, Centra will match those funds. The Cath Lab collected funds from staff throughout cardiology and we now have this to present to you." She handed me an envelope with a card in it.

As I opened the envelope I spoke, "I can't believe ya'll have done this."

Mary said, "Belvia, didn't you have a clue with all these extra people coming in for lunch? What did you think Wayne Lanham was here for? Wayne Lanham is the head of the Chaplaincy program at Centra Health and oversees the Helping Hands program.

"I don't know. It just didn't click with me. I thought Wayne just came to pray for us. God knows we need all the prayers we can get!" Everyone roared with laughter.

I continued on, "You guys have done enough. You've taken care of my family, given gas money to Loren, cleaned my house, sent food and even took care of my flower beds while I've been sick. Except for letting Debbie take the weed-eater to the dead flowers, everything has been wonderful. You didn't need to do this."

Opening the card, I could not believe what I was seeing. There were over two thousand dollars enclosed. I was flooded with a wealth of emotion that I will never be able to explain. My throat locked down. There was so much love there that I couldn't speak to tell them how much I appreciated them. I don't remember too much more about that afternoon, which became a blur of camaraderie and love. I used the money to pay one of the hospital bills I had received that week. Tom asked, "Belvia, when are you coming back to work?' I answered, "Monday," hoping it may be some Monday soon.

A few days later, our lawyer's office called and said they had paid all the bills that had come in on the lien the medical facilities had on the benefit I had gotten from our auto insurance company for our uninsured motorist benefit. They were sending me a check for the remainder minus their fees. This was a wonderful windfall for us. There was enough money to pay off the mortgage. With this, we wouldn't have to be so concerned if I wasn't able to go back to work. There was also enough left over to put some away for Loren's education. Financially, we were not going to be devastated by this accident. I felt God's hand on my shoulder, letting me know that I needed to stop worrying about everything. He was taking care of it. I just needed to have faith.

I had another appointment for a check up by the neurologist who had taken care of me in Lynchburg. My brother, Glen, took me for the visit. The doctor was a kind man who graciously explained to me again the extent of my brain damage and answered all my questions. This he had already done when I was in skilled care at Virginia Baptist, but I didn't remember. He was the first person to give me hope that there could be a solution to some of my visual problems. "After six months have elapsed since your date of injury, I suggest you see an ophthalmologist right here in town who I feel sure can help you with your double vision."

I was ecstatic to hear this. I left that office, arm in arm with my brother, telling him everything the doctor had said. This was the first time I thought that maybe I wouldn't have to go on disability after all. Maybe I would be able to go back to work. Since we were in the neighborhood, Glen and I went to see Mama to tell her the good news. It was a gloriously happy day to be given hope that my condition could continue to improve and life could perhaps come close to being normal again. Learning this was a great relief for me. I realized God was taking care of everything, just like He promises. "The Lord is good, a refuge in times of trouble. He cares for those who trust in Him" (Nahum 1:7, NIV)

Christmas 2002 was a wonderful time of celebration and giving thanks to God for His many blessings over the past few months. I was in awe of everything that was happening. I still thought God was too slow, but had come to understand that His will is worth the wait. We spent time with family and friends that Christmas. We made another trip to Roanoke to have dinner with Bud and Susan who had come

Restoring Spirit

from Texas for the holidays. We walked into the restaurant where all Richard's family was meeting for dinner. We were excitedly greeted by everyone with hugs, kisses, and the joys of prayers answered. We attended the Christmas Eve service at church which was also a moving time of thanksgiving for God's healing power.

As the Christmas holidays passed, I continued to try to patiently wait for the six months of nerve damage healing to be complete. One day, Marie, a wonderful lady from our church, wanted to take me to lunch. It was always good to get out. We met at a little coffee shop on Main Street called R-U-Up. Several other women we knew were already there. We all sat together in the small shop, having a great lunch, talking about our families, and enjoying each others company. Seated facing the window to the street, I could see people scurrying around town to get errands run during their lunch hour. Traffic in town was always busy this time of day on the streets of this quaint small town. Across the street from the coffee shop were two banks. To the left of the banks was Bedford Presbyterian Church, looking very vulnerable without the steeple that had blown off in April. Many of us often wondered when it would ever return. To the right of the banks was an old meeting house that dated back to the pre-civil war time as did Bedford Presbyterian. As I drank my coffee after lunch, talking with these ladies, I noticed a big truck coming up the street toward us from the right. I clasped Marie's arm as the truck got closer, realizing the special cargo it contained.

"Look Marie, our steeple is back!"

"Oh, how wonderful," she said, looking out, patting my hand and smiling.

The steeple was lying on its side, point forward, only a block from home. That vision became a memory that I will never forget. A feeling of wholeness came over me as I felt a personal bonding with that steeple. After lunch, I went home but could not get the steeple off my mind. Later in the afternoon, I returned to town to pay the steeple a special visit. It was sitting upright in the parking lot next to the church awaiting the appointed time to be lifted to its place of honor. It was a day of seeing God at work. He had put me in R-U-Up to witness His will for restoration and coming home in the form of our church steeple. The bond I felt toward the steeple when it was traveling up the street was the understanding that we both had been restored at the same time. As this symbol of the power of the resurrection and ascension of Jesus Christ was being restored to glorify God, so was I. Standing in the parking lot beside the steeple, my response to this understanding was to physically touch it and in doing so, feeling as one with the Father, Son and Holy Spirit. The world kept on turning, the traffic moved down the street as life continued on. Yet for me, that moment in God's hands was frozen in time. It was a personal, private time of Holy Communion with the Trinity.

Just as it was taking time for me to recover, it took time for the steeple and the bell cradle to come to rest on the roof of the church. During that spring as the work was being completed, my recovery was progressing as the time finally came for me to find out what was going to happen with my vision. On the appointed day, I drove myself to the office. Spring was on the way and I enjoyed the drive in the warmth the sun infused into the car. I parked the car in the parking lot of the large office building that housed the physician group of which Dr. Ganzer was a member. I stood beside my car looking at the building, wondering what was in store for me there. I closed my eyes, took a deep breath and told God it was up to Him again.

An attractive young woman walked into the examining room with her right hand out to shake mine and spoke with a positively confident voice, "Hi, I'm Dr. Ganzer. Your neurologist has told me all about you. Let's see what we can do to try to help your vision problems." She did all kinds of visual tests to better define my blind spot, depth of field, and optical needs. She also did measurements from every angle possible to assess my double vision.

"Mrs. Tate, I cannot do anything to improve your blind spot because it was caused by brain damage from your accident. It is in such a position, just off center to the left of your visual field, that I can fully understand the trouble you are experiencing with reading. You actually see very well at a distance and just need glasses for reading. You really have very little depth of field ability right now. That is caused by the alignment of your eyes being askew. While I can't do anything about your blind spot, I may be able to do something to improve your double vision by realigning your eyes. This misalignment is from fourth nerve palsy which has caused one of the muscles in your left eye not to move like it should. What we can do is shorten the muscle to bring your eyes back into better alignment. This will not completely cure your double vision, but will move it to a different area of your visual field that won't bother you as much," Dr. Ganzer explained. "Realignment will also improve your depth of field. I think doing surgery to shorten the muscle in your left eye will improve your visual quality tremendously. If we can move the double vision out of the way, your blind spot will probably become just a nuisance you can adjust to and live with."

"This is great news, Dr. Ganzer. I feel if the double vision can be corrected, I can definitely live with the blind spot. When can we do the surgery?" I questioned.

"It will be a month before I can get you on the surgery schedule at the hospital. In that time, I can do some more extensive testing to calculate how your vision is altered to better understand your surgical needs. Will that work for you?"

"Yes ma'am. I've waited this long; I can wait another month. How long would it be before we know if the surgery is successful?" I asked.

"Sometimes it takes a few days for the eyes to adjust after the surgery. You should know for sure in a week to ten days. I also have a patient, a woman who has had similar surgery. I'll contact her to find out if you can talk to her about her results."

"That'll be great. Let's go ahead and schedule the surgery," I anxiously retorted.

"Alright, we'll do that. Now, if you talk to this woman and decide not to do it, we can talk about it more and do it at another time if you want."

"That won't be necessary. I have full confidence that this is meant to happen."

Since Dr. Ganzer's office is near the hospital, I stopped to see my co-workers before going home to tell them the news of my surgery. While I was still slow moving, I could get from the visitors parking lot to the Cath Lab without having to stop to rest. Improvement was slow, but that didn't matter to me anymore. I was still alive. I could walk and talk and see . . . not good, but I could see. Tom asked, "Belvia, when are you coming back to work?' As always, I answered, "Monday."

During the month before the scheduled eye surgery in March, Dr. Ganzer did measurements and checked angles. She scratched her head a couple of times and measured again. She gave me the telephone number of her patient. She called one of her former mentors with questions, concerned that my measurements were off enough that she wasn't sure what the outcome would be. He told her to go for it anyway. Anything would be better than what I had. I talked to her patient and found this to be very helpful. Her experience was that she could see fine straight ahead now but just had double vision when she

Restoring Spirit

looked straight up. It made for more stars, which could definitely be dealt with.

I was ready for this. I had complete confidence in Dr. Ganzer. I had put myself in God's hands and knew that I would receive what He wanted me to receive. What was received next was snow. It started falling the afternoon before my morning surgery was scheduled. I started praying. "God, if I'm supposed to have this surgery, I know you will make it happen. If not, I'll wait longer if that's how you want it . . . . . Amen."

Richard made it home later that afternoon and assured me that he could get me to the hospital. A short time later, Dr. Ganzer called. "Mrs. Tate, I have a problem. I live at the bottom of a hill and I do not have a four wheel drive vehicle. I'm not going to be able to get out of my street in the morning. The other issue is that if we don't do your surgery tomorrow, it will be another month before I can get you on the surgery schedule."

"Dr. Ganzer, I am going to be at that hospital in the morning. My husband can bring me to get my pre-op work done and then come get you if you're willing to do that. He can even take you home afterwards."

"That would be fine with me. Listen, I've got another patient who really needs to have surgery in the morning. Would you be willing to let me do that surgery first and then do yours? Your husband could take me home while you are in the recovery room."

I turned to Richard to get approval for all these services I was volunteering him for. He nodded his acceptance.

"You've got a deal, Dr. Ganzer."

As I lay in the hospital the next morning waiting for Richard to retrieve Dr. Ganzer, I prayed for God to guide the hands of the doctors and nurses as they worked to provide His healing touch to everyone that day. I felt confident that this surgery was meant to be a positive experience for me. I had no reservations . . . except when the nurse in the OR and Dr. Ganzer were talking about marking the correct site for surgery and how the procedure had changed. I perked up quickly, "I really don't care which eye you mark as long as the surgery is performed on the correct one. Seeing two of my husband every day is getting to be more than I can take." We all laughed as Dr. Ganzer patted my face and told me she knew which eye to work on. As I was being rolled into the operating room, I closed my eyes and prayed silently for the Holy Spirit to empower Dr. Ganzer and thanked Him for bringing us together.

The anesthesiologist was at my head now. "I'm going to put this mask over your face, Mrs. Tate. Just take some slow deep breaths. I'm going to put some medicine in your IV. It might feel cold as it enters your vein. Now count backwards from one-hundred."

"One hundred," my hand felt cold as the drug entered my vein. "Ninety-nine," the anesthesia returned me to the unconscious slumber that I had experienced unknowingly six months before. As I drifted into deep sleep, I felt good knowing God was with us.

"Mrs. Tate, wake up. How are you feeling? OK? You're in the recovery room," the nurse said as I slowly tried to open my eyes. I couldn't see very well because of the salve they had put on my eyes. The nurse was wiping it off. "We are going to take you back to your room as soon as you wake up a little more. Don't be concerned if your vision doesn't seem good yet. Sometimes it takes a few days."

I smiled and groggily told her, "It's alright. I can see enough to know that it's better already. There is only one of you."

I was taken back to the room I had been in before surgery. Loren was there; Richard was taking Dr. Ganzer home. She would see me in three days at her office. I was delighted to be able to see normally again. There would be no days of waiting to see if my vision was better. My vision was already clear; my left eye was just very bloodshot. Loren and I laughed that I wouldn't have to be a pirate anymore, wearing an eye patch to see.

A few days later, my office visit was as joyous for Dr. Ganzer as having my vision back was for me. She couldn't believe the surgery had worked so well.

"I was not at all sure what your result would be, Mrs. Tate. Your measurements were a little unusual. My mentor made suggestions and felt there would be some improvement. We just weren't sure how much. I'm very glad this has turned out so well for you. Mrs. Tate, you are one lucky woman."

I quickly responded, "Luck didn't have a thing to do with it, Dr. Ganzer. God had His hands on yours."

She laughed and said, "Well, that may be true. I really don't know how it happened, but somebody is looking out for you. That's for sure."

I was very blessed and pleased with this surgery. Just as Dr. Ganzer's patient had experienced, I too could see more stars if I looked straight up and to the right or I would see double if I looked straight down and to the left. What the surgery had done was totally switch what I had experienced after the accident. Where I could only see correctly when I looked straight up and straight down, that was now where I saw double. Straight ahead was corrected. What relief and peace of mind this surgical correction gave me. The recovery from the surgery was the quickest I had experienced thus far. I also found out that week before surgery; that my MRSA cultures had finally all come back negative. I was now totally off contact precautions. I stopped by the Cath Lab after my check up with Dr. Ganzer to talk to Mary about coming back to work. I was still not as strong as I would have liked to have been, but that would come with time and exercise. Tom asked, "Belvia, when are you coming back to work?" As always, I answered, "Monday." This time Monday was really here. The time had finally come to start moving closer toward living a normal life again.

I returned to work one week after the eye surgery. I worked part time for a few weeks. I also worked on the committee at church to plan a service and reception for the dedication of our restored steeple. I was in charge of getting an article printed in the local newspaper and running an announcement in the religious section for two weeks before the event. I was also to send invitations to all the churches in our presbytery and the other churches in our area. Jane helped me with that by printing beautiful invitations on her computer. I also wrote the following announcement for our own church newsletter:

4/3/2003 Article for the Bedford Presbyterian Church newsletter.

We are so excited as a church family to see our steeple restored to its proper place and hear our bell joyously ringing the call for all to come worship God. We all have our own stories to tell of how long we patiently waited for the restoration to begin and end. How great it was to see the steeple traveling up Main Street, coming back home like the prodigal son. How we all wanted to touch it while it rested in the parking lot, awaiting return to its place of honor. We will always remember how sweet the sound of hearing the bell ring again after such a long silence.

It is with great joy that we will dedicate to the glory of God our restored steeple on the afternoon of June 1, 2003 at three o'clock. A worship service of thanksgiving and praise will be held in our sanctuary with a reception following in our fellowship hall.

The presence of Bedford Presbyterian's steeple and the ringing of the bell have always been great symbols of our faith in Jesus Christ, not only to us as a congregation, but to the community as well. The community will be invited to join us as we celebrate God's grace in restoring our steeple by lifting it and ourselves up to his service.

I emailed the announcement to Joseph Gaston with the following note:

At first, I wrote how we all wanted to run up and hug the steeple while it was in the parking lot, but I changed it because, while that was what I wanted to do, I couldn't picture a few people doing that!!! And I could have gone on and on about how the restoration of the steeple and bell was symbolic to me personally as its restoration coincided with my own restoration to life as it was before. But then I figured you all didn't want a novel for the newsletter!!! Your input will be greatly appreciated. Joseph's input emailed back to me: "I think you've got a story to tell about restoration."

Joseph had the idea for me to write something to be shared as perhaps a written insert for the program for the steeple dedication service. While I thought it was a good idea, I still was not sure how ready I was to tell my story to others. I still had not shared my Holy Spirit experience with anyone, not even Joseph. It was taking me some time and thought to process all this. I had never been a person who talked about my God experiences. Actually, through the years I had scoffed at them, running my life on my own terms. I wasn't sure I was ready to come out of my comfort zone and expose myself to possible disbelieving listeners. My experience was a story even I would have questioned had it not happened directly to me. Having been a skeptic myself for so many years, it was taking time for me to sort and understand how this experience was affecting me.

God is always using people as seed pods to scatter ideas, thoughts, and messages to others to motivate them into action. What action is that? It is the action of becoming a disciple, of openly responding to all the wonderful things God has done for you. It is telling others about the great love of God that they can have, the same love you have received. I had told Joseph on numerous occasions that he was one of God's seed pods. Here he was planting again, throwing seeds all over me. Seeds don't germinate instantaneously, but often rest in the comfort of warm soil until they are ready to burst forth. I knew God had planted this seed in me for a reason. He had saved my life for a reason. I just wasn't sure what His plan was or how I would respond.

O Giver of every good and perfect gift, if at any time it pleases you to work by my hand, teach me to discern what is my own from what is another's and to render unto you the things that are yours. As all the good that is done on earth, you do yourself, let me ever return to you all the glory. Let me as a pure crystal transmit all the light you pour upon me. -John Wesley, 1703-1791 (Bideaux, p. 119)

Treasure Forever

Personally, I am not very enthusiastic about jumping into water that I cannot see through. I want to know what is hiding there; I want a glimpse of what might happen when I go in. Having faith in God is sometimes like jumping into water you are not sure of. Yet, you just have to go ahead and jump, trusting that God will make the way clear for you. That proverbial "leap of faith" others tell you to take is often easier said than done. Sometimes it takes us time to get used to this new revelation of trust and faith that goes along with the gift of God's presence in our lives.

"But the Counselor, the Holy Spirit, whom the Father will send in my name, he will teach you all things, and bring to your remembrance all that I have said to you. Peace I leave with you; my peace I give to you; not as the world gives do I give to you. Let not your hearts be troubled, neither let them be afraid" (John 14:26-27, <u>The Oxford Annotated Bible</u>, p.1307).

The next year and a half was spent getting back into the routine of living a normal life. My relationship with God was growing stronger and stronger. I attended an Alpha Course presented by Joseph at our church during this time. One of the ladies talked of an experience of feeling a sensation of peace flow over her at a time when she had prayed for God's intervention in her life. Her story moved me to tears and I shared my Holy Spirit experience with this small group of women and Joseph. This was the first time I had told anyone of my experience when I was in the hospital.

After taking this course, I felt I had a better understanding of the power of God's wonderful grace. Thoughts and memories of how God had worked in the lives of the people I loved and in my own life were constantly popping into my head. Why are all these memories flooding me now? What am I supposed to do with all these ideas that keep invading my head? A gift of understanding was being bestowed on me and it was time for me to stand up and shout about what had happened to me. In subtle, yet decisive ways, God was showing me what He wanted of me all along. He just needed to give me a little nudge to get me going.

One day in the fall of 2004, I stopped at the post office for stamps before going to Lynchburg. Christine, a dear sweet lady from our church family and one of the leaders of the Presbyterian Women, was there and started talking to me about the upcoming Presbyterian Women's Retreat. She asked me if I might be interested in giving a testimony during the program. I told her I would think about it and let her know in a few days. She finished her business; we said our good-byes. As I left the post office and was walking to my car, Christine stopped her car to tell me something else. She said, "Belvia, I just wanted to let you know that the theme of the retreat is *He Touched Me*. I thought you might want to know that to help you know what you might talk about."

I thanked her and she drove away. I got in my car, drove out of the parking lot and cried all the way to Lynchburg. Thinking of what I had to tell filled my heart with tears of great joy and thanksgiving. It was time for me to speak up to tell others of my experience and what God could do for anyone who will give their life to Him. I knew then, I had to accept the invitation to speak.

On the day of the retreat, I was very nervous about standing in front of all these women to tell my story. I had talked to Loren earlier in the week about my fears. She, of course, encouraged me and reminded me that most of these women were friends of mine and knew me well. They loved me already and would still love me no matter how nervous I was. Before leaving home for the church, I went to God in prayer:

"Heavenly Father, I thank you for the opportunity to tell of your gracious gifts to others. But just like so many of your chosen disciples, I feel weak and unworthy. I am not a good public speaker and I have had terrible stage fright ever since I was a child. I always lose my place and my hands shake so badly that I can't hide it. I also start crying and then I can't talk at all. I ask that You be with me today as I tell my story and make it an inspiration to all who hear it to learn more about understanding the power of Your love. Please help me not shake so much and keep me from crying. Amen."

When it was my turn to speak, I walked to the podium with my notes in hand. As I placed the notes on the podium, my hands were shaking as I had expected them to. So I started by telling the women about the prayer I had made to God before I got there. "I'm not sure why God has put me in this position to speak to you. But as I become more and more Presbyterian in my theological beliefs, I know there is a reason for everything. I've been praying a lot before coming here. I know speaking in front of you ladies is what God wants me to do, but I'm not very good at this sort of thing and I hope you will bear with me as I try to tell this story.

I've been having trouble getting this story organized and condensed because there are so many little pieces to this puzzle. My husband Richard handed me the *Power for Living* flyer that Mr. Brandt gave him last Sunday morning here at church. One of the devotions was about Job. Within it was quoted an excerpt from the book <u>When Life Gets Tough</u> by Rabbi Kushner. It was just what I needed to get me focused. Kushner states, "Life is not fair. The wrong people get sick and the wrong people get robbed and the wrong people get killed in wars and in accidents . . . suffering is an inevitable part of life. Misfortune never leaves us where it finds us. The pain will one day cease. But what we learn in these dark experiences is our treasure forever" (Garpiepy, p. 8). That is what has happened to me."

My shaking hands becoming steadier, I then proceeded to tell them about that fateful night of the accident that I don't remember much about and waking up two months later to realize I had been near death. I also told them how many wonderful things have come from this tragic event . . .

—A lot of people learned that the power of prayer is an awesome force . . .

—Many who knew me learned to believe in miracles . . .

—I hope all of the youth in this town who know me learned never to drink and drive . . .

—As a Resident Advisor at Hollins University, Loren always gives her residents the "My mother was almost killed by a drunk driver" speech to deter them from this behavior . . .

—My sister-in-law has come back into our lives after a long separation . . .

—And I have a new perspective and appreciation of life . . .

Restoring Spirit

I closed my testimony by sharing a poem my daughter, Loren, wrote. She gets some of her best inspiration under stress. She wrote this poem and put it in one of the scrapbooks she made for me of my get well cards. It is titled *Refinement*.

Cleanse my soul
Make me whole
Usher me down

Torch my fears
Let me burn
Hold me near
Search my shadows
Know me better
Than I do

Purify my thoughts
Light the dark
Polish my scars

Smooth these edges
Down these walls
Melt my misconceptions

Reduce to ashes
Sift the pain
Let me remain

I was, by God's grace, allowed to remain as Loren's poem petitions. Yet, I remained a changed person. I was reduced to ashes and was still kept on this earth to be God's servant. This experience, being brought from the darkness into the light of God's love by the power of the touch of the Holy Spirit as the energy courses through the body, is the overwhelming act of God's refinement. It was the torching of my fears, the polishing of my scars, the melting of my misconceptions, and the cleansing of my soul. The Belvia that remains will go through the rest of this life with my hand reaching for God's, as He leads the way. And just like the passage I shared with you earlier . . . "what I learned in these dark experiences . . . to put my total trust in God . . . is my treasure forever."

"Sickness is not being beaten up by God but an opportunity for promise and healing. Its cause may be inexplicable, yet it can become the moment when God brings wholeness into your life" (Morgan, meditation 26).

Talking about the unclean woman in the crowd who touched Jesus' robe to be healed of her sickness "John Sanford says that 'her illness was an essential step on her way to wholeness . . . . If she had been cured by well-intentioned doctors, she would have overcome her malady, but she would not have been changed and renovated in soul and spirit as well as in body." (Morgan, meditation 1).

How true this is, especially from the point of view of having lived this experience. Surely, I wanted the healing of my body. I wanted to get back to my life of working, gardening, and taking care of my home. The medical staff that helped care for me facilitated that. I did learn to walk again. I learned to adjust to my visual problems. I was reading and driving again after a long time of uncertainty. Even though I would never fully return to the physical status I was in before the accident, I did become self sufficient again. I did go back to work, gardening, and doing all those domestic chores, not as well maybe but doing them anyway. After all the physical trials my body has endured from my scoliosis to this accident, the wholeness of my body is inconsequential when compared to the wholeness of my soul in right relationship with God, the Father, Son, and Holy Spirit. Jesus speaks to me just as he did the woman touching the hem of His robe, "Daughter, be of good comfort; thy faith hath made thee whole" (Matthew 9:22, The Holy Bible, New Testament, p. 10).

I used to tell people that I believed there was a power out there greater than me. I knew that man was not the creator of the earth and the heavens. I wasn't really sure what that power was, but I believed it was out there somewhere. The power really had no control over my life. I felt that all the stories of the Bible, Koran, and the theological framework of all religions were the creation of man. Even having gone back to church in the late 1990's, I was still skeptical of much of what was written. I studied world religions in college and felt I had a pretty good understanding of the backgrounds and premises of the major ones. I have always been open minded and accepting of other people's beliefs and religious practices, mainly because I just wasn't sure of any of it.

Now, I don't just believe that greater power is out there somewhere, I know He is there. And He's not just out there; He is everywhere. I cannot say that I know this because I have seen God as a defined entity with specific shape and form. Yet I have seen Him and felt His presence time and time again. He is in all of us. He is in me, in my heart, in my spirit. I do see Him everyday in the eyes, smiles, and actions of other people I encounter. He works through me for others and through others for me.

A few months after giving my testimony to the Presbyterian Women's group, I read an article from Presbyterians Today titled Treasures of Darkness by Kristine A. Haig. The author was speaking of people who have been through great mourning or suffering finding a profound spiritual knowledge.

"... there was a spiritual quality that was like a kind of shining—a radiance of faith and trust that was almost palpable ... there poured out from them a powerful confidence in the goodness of God, an assurance of the mystery of life that does not end with our deaths.

Perhaps this was because they had moved from believing to knowing—from trusting *in theory* that God will not desert us in our need, to descending to the very depths of suffering and finding God there ...

Not everyone who experiences loss will automatically have this kind of bone-deep God-knowing. But once experienced, it is a treasure of the greatest value.

When I meet people who through hard experience have come by this profound trust in God, I am reminded of the luminous words of the prophet Isaiah, who speaks of "the treasures of darkness and riches hidden in secret places" (The Oxford Annotated Bible, Is. 45:3). It is indeed a spiritual treasure to know the real and reliable presence of God with heart, as well as with head ...

Life is a test of endurance; hope only a vague memory. And then, eventually, there comes a day when we notice the beauty of a bird's song again, perhaps for the first time in months. We are aware that our dinner tastes good, our children are gifted and loving, and there is something we are looking forward to in the future.

Sometimes we have been carried along on the prayers of others for a long time, and then find we have recovered the capacity to pray for ourselves.

When we can say, as Christian says in the spiritual classic, The Pilgrim's Progress, "I have touched the bottom, and it is sound"—when we know that there is a bottom, and that it will not give way—there is a kind of comfort and assurance. To know the companionship of

Christ with us at that bottom is a great blessing. There is treasure in our darkness and riches in the secret hidden places of our pain" (Haig, p.6).

I used to fear death. I feared the uncertainty of not knowing what exists past this life, if anything. Now, that fear has left me forever. I cannot say that I saw a bright white light while I was unconscious that was drawing me to Heaven. Actually, what I saw was more akin to what I thought was hell with the Beetle Juice characters I was seeing in my drugged state. Knowing that God had sent the Holy Spirit to me to calm my fears and lead me through this trial is what took my fear from me. What could have been disastrous instead became wondrous. Romans 14: 8-9 says "As long as we have life we are living to the Lord; or if we give up our life it is to the Lord; so if we are living, or if our life comes to an end, we are the Lord's. And for this purpose Christ went into death and came back again, that he might be the Lord of the dead and of the living" (The Oxford Annotated Bible, p. 1374). There is no longer need to fear or worry about what death will bring. God is big enough to take care of all that. All you need do is trust in Him.

Once you experience and accept the living water of God's love pouring over you, you cannot help but see how He is working in your life and the lives of others. You learn that it is through people just like you that God sends messages, teaches lessons, and shows the way to His intentions. Just like the waves of the ocean continue to break on the shore and the undertow takes the water back out to sea, so does life continue to ebb and flow. Life does not stop to allow you to get accustomed to your new found faith, but keeps coming at you with crashing waves. Yet once God's love is understood, the waves become less overwhelming because you know He is always with you. He will help guide you through anything if you will only let Him.

Epilogue
August, 2007

The waters of Stoney Creek in Bedford County still flow from the Blue Ridge Mountains on their journey to the Atlantic Ocean, ever changing course and character. So does our life continue from one day to the next with obstacles of joy and trials. Does my experience with such a physical and spiritual encounter with the Holy Spirit mean I have all the answers for what life is all about? No. Does it mean I'm going to always get it right? No. Does it mean my trials are over? No, not hardly.

All of the obstacles we face, good or bad, and how we approach and respond to them are what make us who we are, mold our thoughts and emotions, and either bring us to a better understanding of what God is all about or make us turn away. Yet, even in our efforts to turn away, God is still there for us. He's watching over us, trying to show us the best path to take. We are often stubborn and self-absorbed thinking we are stronger and more in control than we really are. At those times, God will often allow us to fall down so low that we fear we might never survive. He at times must put us in a position that finally shows us that there are situations that we cannot control. It took getting knocked down to a point near death and surviving that made me realize God's forgiveness was there for me, no matter what I had done in the past or how unworthy I felt. All I had to do was merely accept God's gracious gift of forgiveness through Jesus Christ, allow the Holy Spirit to touch me, take His hand and let Him be the leader.

I still stray from his guidance. Life gets busy sometimes and I forget that I need to keep God in the forefront of everything I do. I still get frustrated when things don't go as I want them to. God's timing and mine are still not always in sync. He is still trying to teach me patience. I am a difficult student. Yet, when I forget to put God first, He is always gracious enough to nudge me in some fashion to remind me of Him. A friend will send a card. An unexpected flower will bloom. A song will have a phrase in it that I hear above all else or I'll get goose bumps singing the anthem with the choir. That happened a few weeks ago.

Over the years my scoliosis in my spine had progressed. My physician and I had been talking about my need for surgery for a year and a half. I decided from the beginning to put the situation in God's hands. It took several months to get on the physician's surgery schedule. I had four more months to wait. I made up my mind to be watchful and patient. I felt God had led me to this physician at this time. If He wanted me to have this surgery, it would happen without a hitch. If He didn't want me to have it, He would put up some kind of roadblock to stop it.

No roadblocks occurred. My employer worked with me for my medical leave and how I would be able to work when I returned. All my medical testing was good. I had been walking and working out for months. I was more fit than I had been in years. Everything fell into place like it was meant to be that way from the start.

On the Sunday before the surgery, I sang in the choir for what would be the last time for several months. The anthem we sang could not have been replaced by any other for what I needed to hear on that particular Sunday. It was *Who At My Door is Standing?*

Restoring Spirit

> Who at my door is standing,
> There patiently drawing near,
> Who entrance is demanding?
> Whose is the voice I hear?
> Sweetly the tones are falling:
> "Now open the door for me!
> If thou wilt heed my calling,
> I will abide with thee."
>
> Within, the rooms are darken'd,
> All filled with dust and sin;
> How shameful, how unworthy
> For Christ to enter in.
> Yet, the tones are falling:
> "Now open the door for me!
> If thou wilt heed my calling,
> I will abide with thee."
>
> Door of my heart, I hasten!
> Thee will I open wide.
> Though he rebuke and chasten,
> He shall with me abide.
> Sweetly the tones are falling;
> "Now open the door for me!"
> Lord God, I hear thee calling,
> Come now, abide with me.
> Dear Lord, abide with me!

As we finished singing, goose bumps rose on my arms. I felt the Holy Spirit touching me once again to let me know that He was with me. It wasn't as powerful a touch as I had 5 years previously. But the timing and meaning were just as dramatic as before. He was telling me, "Belvia, you're doing the right thing. This is what I want for you. No matter what happens, you will be fine." And I am fine because I am the Lord's.

God is good, all the time. All the time, God is good. Amen.

Works Cited

Bideaux, Rene O., Compiler, <u>A Book of Personal Prayer,</u> copyright 1997, Upper Room Books, Nashville, TN.

Brueggemann, Walter, <u>Awed to Heaven, Rooted in Earth: Prayers of Walter Brueggemann,</u> copyright 2003, Augsburg Fortress Press, Box 1209, Minneapolis, MN 55440.

Garpiepy, Henry, The *Bright Path: That which I was afraid of is come unto me*, <u>Power for Living</u>, Volume 63, Number 1, October 10, 2004, SP Publications, Colorado Springs, CO, copyright 2004.

Haig, Kristine A., *Treasures of darkness*, <u>Presbyterians Today</u>, July/August 2005.

Morgan, Richard L., <u>From Grim to Green Pastures</u>, copyright 1994, Upper Room Books, Nashville, TN.

Slade, Mary, "Who At My Door Is Standing," copyright 1875, arr. K. Lee Scott, copyright 1985 by Hinshaw Music Inc., PO Box 470, Chapel Hill, NC 27514.

<u>The Bible Promise Book,</u> Barbour Publishing, Inc., Uhrichsville, OH, all quotes from <u>The Holy Bible: New International Version</u>, The International Bible Society, copyright 1973, 1978, 1984, Zondervan Publishing House.

The Catholic Study Bible: New American Bible, copyright 1990, Oxford University Press, Inc., 200 Madison Avenue, New York, NY 10016.

The Holy Bible, *King James Version*, The World Publishing Company, 223 West 10th Street, Cleveland, OH.

The New Oxford Annotated Bible, Revised Standard Version, Expanded Edition, Oxford University Press, New York, NY, copyright 1973, 1977.

The Oxford Annotated Bible, Revised Standard Version, College Edition, Oxford University Press, New York, NY, copyright 1962.

About the Author

Belvia Holt Tate has worked as a Radiologic Technologist and Cardiovascular Professional for forty years. She enjoys photography, painting, and reading in her spare time. She lives with her family in Virginia.

About the Book

Restoring Spirit has taken eleven years to bring to publication. The bulk of it was written in 2004. Putting all these memories and feelings in writing was very therapeutic for me in the aftermath of the accident. But the accident was becoming the major event in my life that everything was chronologically placed around. I needed to put it to rest and move on to my future. I did return to it for a short period in 2007, when the Epilogue was written as the end of the story.

Knowing that God would take it for His use someday in his own time, it is now ready to be shared.